Discovering
God's
Favor

Dear Josh,

I appreciate your servant's heart. It is always a joy to serve with you.

Merry Christmas,

John Gillette

LARGE PRINT EDITION

Discovering God's Favor

A TRIPLETS FAITH JOURNEY

John F. Gillette

Author of Discovering God's Presence

Chapbook Press

Chapbook Press

Schuler Books

2660 28th Street SE

Grand Rapids MI 49512

www.schulerbooks.com

Discovering God's Favor - A Triplets Faith Journey

ISBN: 9781943359141

eBook ISBN: 9781943359158

Library of Congress Control Number: 2015951687

Cover art and Graphics design - Jerry Montague, Montague Design Group, Inc.

Cover Design ©2015 - Jerry Montague

Editor - Carrie Holstege

Typist - Joy E. Gillette

This book was written in honor of my parents John G. Gillette and Mary H. Gillette.

I am **thankful** for their witness of God's grace. I **appreciate** their dedication to God's word. I am **grateful** for their discipling. I am **encouraged** with their faithfulness. I am **blessed** to be their son.

Wonderful Grace of Jesus
2 Corinthians 8:9

The songwriter has written "Wonderful grace of Jesus, greater than all my sin. How shall my tongue describe it? Where shall its praise begin? Taking away my burden, setting my spirit free; for the wonderful grace of Jesus reaches me." *Discovering God's Favor* is my spiritual autobiography. It is the life of a triplet, a triplet that was born with a triple desire to serve God through music, ministry and mentoring. He was driven by passion, independence and diversity. It uses key hymns and spiritual song phrases to introduce each chapter's theme. It follows with a devotional scripture. Biographical illustrations will show how the Biblical truth may mold life. God is working. Is he working in your life? Look at your life closely and you may be surprised and be drawn closer to him. Through reading my testimony, the hope is that you will know God better.

I have been blessed with a deep desire and have been given reliable resources to push me forward. Some people have a problem with a lack of interest in what I am writing about. Some people will diligently search for an answer and remain perplexed with all the hindrances of the day. Some people are led down the wrong path by religious fanatics. Some people are just plain blind to the truth.

I have been blessed with having parents who have been led in the belief that Jesus Christ is Savior and Lord. They have pursued every means to instruct me in the way, the truth and the life. As a matter of fact, the thing I remember most is that my grandmother would sit in her rocking chair, praying and reading her Bible. My parents continued the journey discipling me in such a way that my heroes would be preachers, evangelists and missionaries. Today, I listen to their sermons and I can remember their faces and platform deportment.

I have been blessed to rely upon a belief system

that is in a person who is God. Biblical authority has not been doubted because when I mix the Word with faith, it works. This absolute truth has become a solid rock for me. I have studied it, have taught it, have tested it, and have looked at the haters of the truth, the ignorant of the truth, the scholars and even believers that have a problem with it during difficult times in their lives. I have been blessed to be secure in my doctrinal beliefs in Jesus Christ They have been sound from the beginning. What I believed in my childhood, I believe now in my senior years.

Belief in God has become steadfast in my life because I have grown in his grace. I know a lot of people that are not secure and I think they have to let go of self. The trinity of self - me, myself and I - are getting in the way. I have been blessed to live with the inner courage to follow Jesus. The Holy Spirit indwells me. He is my witness that God the Father has chosen me, God the Son has purchased me and God the Holy Spirit has sealed me. The more I pursue him, the more I realize that he is pursuing me. The holy urge is always prompting me as I allow the Holy Scriptures to penetrate my soul. I have been blessed with his benefits. Christianity is practical and it gives me a life that is abundant and overflowing. Even during unrest, worry, confusion and confrontation, God makes his presence felt. I know he is near because I am living in the moment with him. The Bible says, "God is able to make all grace abound to you so that in all things at all times, having all that you need, you will abound in every good work" (2 Corinthians 9:8). *Discovering God's Favor* is filled with God's graciousness. Grace is what God does for me, not what I do for God or for myself. Salvation is God's greatest gift and my greatest need. God gives and I receive. Grace is God's channel for me to receive God's free gift (Hebrews 11:6). Faith is the means for me to experience grace. I am his 'workmanship' (Ephesians 2:10). Christ is for me (grace); it is Christ in me (faith) and Christ through me (works). I will 'abound' because God is working through his grace. When the kingdom of God is placed first, the temporal needs are included. I have to practice righteousness. How do I do that? ..by constant seeking. This means that my dominant concern is spiritual, not material. It means I have a continued hunger and thirst after righteousness. It is setting my affection on things above. It is seeking holiness. It is the desire to know God better.

The priority is to 'think correctly'. To 'think correctly' means to think biblically. I have encircled my life with these thoughts concerning grace. "And the word became flesh and dwelt among us, and we saw his glory, glory as of the only begotten from the Father full of grace and truth" (John 1:14). In the Scripture there are numerous demonstrations of grace. It is to "extend favor or kindness to one who doesn't deserve it and can never earn it." God came to earth through the goodness of his heart to "stoop down" and give us a forgiveness and acceptance into his kingdom. As I travel through my spiritual autobiography, it is God who provides salvation and has chosen me to live a holy life. He did this not because I deserved it but because that was his plan long before the world began – to show his love and kindness to me through Christ Jesus (2 Timothy 1:9). I have been eternally justified on the basis of grace. It is a gift and is absolutely free. I cannot boast. It is by grace through faith (Ephesians 2:1-9). As I travel through my spiritual autobiography, it is God that provides peace (Romans 5:1).

My sovereign God declares me righteous even

while I am in a sinning state. That transaction begins a process of growth toward maturity. It is progressive. Day by day, I learn to honor Christ. I am grateful to God for repentance, forgiveness, belief, justification, justice and grace. As I travel through my spiritual autobiography, it is God that provides my needs. "For the Lord God is a sun and shield; the Lord gives grace and glory. No good thing does he withhold from those who walk uprightly" (Psalm 84:11). His grace is observed through each chapter. The "Wonderful Grace of Jesus" provides: Victory, Belief, Love, Focus, Redemption, Transformation, Faith, Renewal, Guidance, Fellowship, Trust, Success, Order, Dependence, Desire, Silence, Relationship, Submission, Peace, Reliance, Blessings, Intimacy, Comfort, Enablement, Glory, Hope, Communion, Intervention, Service, Confidence, Security, Submission, and Peace.

As I travel through my faith journey, it is God that provides undeserved and yet unconditional love. "But by the grace of God I am what I am, and his grace toward me did not prove vain" (1 Corinthians 15:10). I am not interested in this world's ego-centered kingdom but rather the kingdom of heaven

(Matthew 6:33). I challenge you to write your own spiritual autobiography. Share your own personalized statement regarding how God's grace affects your life. I hope I can, along with the New Testament writers, mention the grace of God in both my greetings and my closing remarks. I have been blessed by his grace, that "Wonderful Grace of Jesus." Join me on my life's journey!

TESTIMONIAL INDEX

x

TOPICAL INDEX

ONE

ONWARD CHRISTIAN SOLDIERS
Ephesians 6:10-20

The songwriter has written, "Onward Christian Soldiers! Marching as to war, with the cross of Jesus going on before. Christ, the royal master leads against the foe." As a teenager and young adult, this song was a favorite. It was a fantastic trumpet solo. You can imagine the soldiers marching. The single, triple and gruppetto tonguing would take you into victory. I played it many times to praise the Lord, and every time I was challenged to "stand up for Jesus" and go forward into battle. The low tones brought a solid foundation and the piercing high tones would scream out to get your attention.

I have begun with "forward into battle, with

Christ's promises which can never fail" because my life can be traced through history with wars. Matthew 24:6-7 says "and ye shall hear of wars and rumors of wars: see that ye be not troubled: for all these things must come to pass but the end is not yet. For nations shall rise against nations..." I'm glad that Jesus Christ has been my family's "light and salvation, whom shall I fear?" "He shall hide me in His pavilion" (Ps. 27:1, 3-5).

My birth took place when World War II started. On August 31, 1939, Hitler and the Nazis staged a Polish attack on a minor German radio station in order to justify a German invasion of Poland. On September 1, Hitler declared war on Poland, and France and Britain had a defense pact with Poland. This forced France and Britain to declare war on Germany which they did on September 3. The Soviet Union invaded Poland from the east on September 17. The war in Europe was under full swing. The war in the Pacific was plotted by Japan and an Imperial takeover of Asia was underway. I was born along with my sisters on December 17, 1939. *The Grand Rapids Press* and *The Herald* newspapers would carry news of the war. At the same time for several years, the papers would also carry highlights of "the Christmas babies - triplets born." Birth is always a miracle. In my case, it was unique, amazing and God-touched. My parents didn't expect triplets. Their first baby weighed the same amount as the trio did. They were born at home due to the winter storm that caused everything to stop but birth. We were born in an upstairs apartment. Our first bassinette was a chest of drawers. Milk was provided because of publicity we had in the newspapers. We were the only set of triplets born in our birth year. We are one of the oldest set recorded in the official records in our county.

The act of creation is amazing. "And the Lord God formed man of the dust of the ground, and breathed into his nostrils the breath of life; and man became a living soul" (Genesis 2:7). This verse reveals to us that the body was made of the dust of the ground, that the spirit came from the breath of God, and that the combination produced the soul. Man is a soul; therefore, he has his own identity. The soul is self-conscientiousness. His personality is discovered through his intellect, emotion and will. His body is where the soul and spirit live. It is wonderfully made and has a story of its own to tell. The breath of God produced life and is the very nucleus of life. The Bible says, "For the Word of God is living and active, sharper than any two-edged sword. It penetrates even to the dividing of soul and spirit, joints and marrow, and it judges the thoughts and attitudes of the heart" (Hebrews 4:12 NIV).

In my childhood years, we would feel the effects of the Korean War occurring June 25, 1950 and a cease fire on July 27, 1953. This was a civil war between states of North Korea and South Korea that were created out of World War II. The principle support on the side of the North Korean communists was the People's Republic of China. The United Nations forces, primarily from the United States, supported South Korea. There was never a "real" end of the war. The conflict still technically persists to this day. It's hard to believe that at ten years of age, while pulling my red wagon down the street to a friend's house to play, that many casualties would be added to a list from a war dubbed the *Forgotten War* or the *Unknown War*. The United States would experience 33,685 battle deaths, 2,830 non-battle deaths, and 17,730 deaths of personnel outside the Korean theatre.

There were also 8,142 United States personnel listed as *Missing in Action* during the war. This wouldn't account for the thousands from the enemy or other countries killed in action. The Korean War was the first armed confrontation of the Cold War and set the standard for many later conflicts. It created the idea of a limited war where the two superpowers would fight in another country making the people in that nation suffer the bulk of the destruction and death involved in the war between such large nations. The superpowers avoided descending into an all-out war with one another as well as the mutual use of nuclear weapons.

As I grew up into my teens and early twenties, the Berlin Wall surrounding West Berlin was built. More tension began to build. The Soviet Union had missiles that would be launched against Europe but U.S. missiles were capable of striking the entire Soviet Union. Cuba was only ninety miles off the coast of Florida. In April 1962, the Soviet Union conceived the idea of placing intermediate-range missiles in Cuba. The Cuban Missile Crisis was the closest the world ever came to a nuclear war. This was a scary time as I had just graduated from college with a degree in Theology (BTh). The draft was on my door step. I consulted about the possibility of auditioning for one of the military bands or completing my studies and joining the service as a Chaplain. Tension finally began to ease when the Soviet Union announced to dismantle missile installations and the United States agreed not to invade Cuba.

You would think, hopefully, that peace would be around the corner. Let's get on with the life goals and pursue happiness, but no such luck. Vietnam problems would create issues that demanded some answers. The communist north and the democratic south were in a battle for reunification. Three United States Presidents became involved with this war. One President chose a middle route to follow, which was a limited partnership with South Vietnam. The second President chose to follow a plan of military intervention and sent combat troops. The third President would expand the war into Laos and Cambodia. A peace accord would be signed to end hostilities between the United States and Democratic Republic of Vietnam. The Paris Peace Agreement did not end the conflict in Vietnam. The communist forces captured Saigon. A promise to not abandon

South Vietnam was agreed upon if certain peace accords would be signed. The promise was never kept.

The 60's and 70's were years of confusion, unrest, alternative thinking, turmoil, situation ethics, and less than a little genuine spiritual interest from a Biblical point of view. During those years I began pursuing a lifelong learning journey. I have never become studious for money, fame, prestige or any other reasons like that. I would study because I wanted to know more and be able to be more competent in what I happened to be doing at the time. I was always ready to learn new things and to keep my passionate, independent and diversified style of life. The studies would differ according to my interest which was pastoral, educational and para church leadership. Those years brought many possibilities in education. I always tried to balance the traditional with the alternative and the distance learning with the classroom. I wrote my own curriculum and I would sit under knowledgeable scholars. The years were exciting and adventurous. They laid the foundation for a future doctorate in Philosophy (PhD.), Biblical Christianity and a doctorate in ministries (DMin) with organizational development.

After World War II, the Korean War, Cuban Crisis and the Vietnam War, we would be faced with trouble in the Middle East and always trouble-conflict-unresolved issues in the East. In my adulthood, the Persian Gulf War would be on every television set. The power and speed to save little Kuwait would take place and even now the Iraq War that continues endlessly. Is World War III around the corner? We live in days of war. The invisible war is everywhere. Against the body, Satan brings the temptations of the flesh. Against the soul, he brings the temptations of the world. Against the spirit, he chooses to come himself or sends one of his lesser agents. Attacks will be made and conflicts will continue.

It all started when Satan and sin entered the universe. God created the earth and the heavens with His word. Lucifer-Satan announced that he had to take possession of them for himself. By the simple word of God, the heavens and the earth toppled into judgment. In that same moment, Satan got his first mouthful of dirt. Dust in the mouth is a perfect figure for defeat and destruction. Satan had lifted himself toward heaven in a surge of awful desire to be like

God, and his mouth was filled with dust. Every man or woman who wishes to be independent of God in Christ is in the path of Lucifer-Satan. Satisfaction is not to be found outside of God as he is revealed in Jesus Christ, with obedience to his will.

We can have victory in our war. We are able to abstain from temptation to the flesh (body). We are to believe and not conform to the world (soul). We are to resist Satan (spirit). The key words are flight, faith and fight. In my senior years, I'm learning to be a soldier that is marching with the cross of Jesus. I will conquer and be victorious as I daily put on God's armor. I would start every instrumental solo with scripture. With "Onward Christian Soldiers" I would use Ephesians 6:10: "My brothers, be strong in the Lord and in the power of his might." The power is found in the three words that represent Christ: 1) His death – strong, 2) His resurrection – power, and 3) His ascension - might. The trio would produce Pentecostal power. We can't fail when we allow this to work in our lives. If we want to stand, we must "Put on the whole armor of God" (Ephesians 6:11). We have an invisible conflict. It is a spiritual battle with the "Prince of the power of the air" (Ephesians

2:2). The strategy is to live life with integrity, purity, victory, security and the Word. The foundation is truth. It will hold everything together. Satan is a liar (John 8:44) and Jesus is the truth (John14:6). With integrity, we will have a clear conscience.

Our righteousness is received through Jesus (2 Cor. 5:21). The accuser, Satan, is a specialist in deception. Bad behavior breeds open opportunity for Satan. Our conduct must not give him any space. We must always have an attitude of repentance, confession, forgiveness and renewal. Our focus should always be on victory. Satan creates doubt and confusion but Jesus is our peace (Ephesians 2:14). We must march toward victory. We have divine support. He provides it right at the moment we need it. Faith is our shield. It will quench all the fiery darts of the wicked. Satan will try us with all sorts of things but Jesus gives us faith (Galatians 2:20). Keep in mind, "but ye are not in the flesh but in the spirit, if so be that the Spirit of God dwell in you..." (Romans 8:9-10). We are secure in him. He is doing the battle for us.

As we become rooted, built up and established in faith that Jesus provides us with, we will conquer.

Satan likes to play tricks with our minds, but we are complete in Jesus when our mind stays focused. Salvation in Christ Jesus is our confidence and security. Jesus used the Scripture against the enemy "as it is written" (Luke 4:1-13), we are able to do the same. Keep marching forward as Christian soldiers.

TWO

ONLY TRUST HIM
Matthew 11:28-30

The songwriter has written, "Come every soul by sin oppressed, there's mercy with the Lord; and he shall surely give you rest by trusting in His Word. Only Trust Him, Only Trust Him, He will save you." He will give you rest. Have you read Jesus' words, "Come unto me" in Matthew 11:28-30? Have you heard His sweet, deep, sensitive, authentic, bold, eternal, and changing words?

"Come unto me" is an open invitation. Let's discover what Jesus means with such awesome words. We better start with a little background. The Gospel according to Matthew gives a view of the life of Jesus. Most likely, the early accounts were passed on verbally in the Aramaic language and then recorded in Greek manuscripts dating from A.D. 60 to A.D. 90. Matthew emphases the Old Testament preparation for the gospel and makes it an ideal "bridge" from the Old to the New Testament. Matthew, the Hebrew tax collector, writes for the Hebrew mind. He tells us that Jesus is the Messiah foretold by Old Testament prophets. He starts with the genealogy of Jesus. The coming of Christ to the earth has been anticipated from the beginning. In the early days of human history, God chose one family line, that of Abraham, and later on another family with the Abrahamic family, that of David, to be the family through which His son would make entrance into the world.

Miracles, lessons learned and many activities have already taken place, but now we have come to chapter eleven of Matthew, verses 28-30, to think about Jesus' sweet words "Come unto me." The purpose of the gospel is to present the good news of the Redeemer-Savior. Jesus is the Messiah of Israel, the Son of God, and the Savior of the World.

"Come unto me" are life-changing words but they can't be heard by our sinful, rebellious and stubborn minds without a sovereignly bestowed spiritual awakening. We read of a free offer to all in verses 28-30 and a divine initiative in verse 27. I'm so glad that the Holy Spirit convicts us and the sovereign work of God is at hand so that we can trust our spirit, soul and body to Jesus Christ. Authority and confidence are found in verse 27. "All things are delivered unto me of my father: and no man knoweth the Son, but the Father: neither knoweth any man the Father, save the Son, and he to whom so ever the Son will reveal Him." Jesus is the way initiated by the Father. "My Father" reveals Jesus' absolute equality; He is the "only begotten Son." Personal knowledge of the Father through the Son with the assistance of the Holy Spirit will develop assurance and authority in living. How does genuine conversion take place? The songwriter says, "Only Trust Him" and the text continues with the answer.

"All ye that labor and are heavy laden" are words that describe our condition. If we are going to hear God's call through Jesus, we have to be in a condition of humility. The labor and burden has brought us to exhaustion and just plain sweat. We have to lay our load at Jesus' feet. Trying to save ourselves will not work, doing all the good works will not do it, a guilty conscience will not do it, but a broken heart realizing total dependence is necessary. We will hear his voice "Come unto me" when we recognize our sinful condition. In the present condition we don't measure up to God's standards. In my childhood, I responded to Jesus. I had been singing with my sisters at a Bible Conference. On the way home, our mother asked if we would like to ask Jesus into our hearts. We knew the gospel story. Because of sin, we were separated from God (Romans 3:23), and the penalty for sin is death (Romans 6:23). Thankfully that penalty for sin was paid by Jesus Christ (Romans 5:8). If we repent of the sin (acknowledge need), then confess and trust Jesus as Lord and Savior (accept Jesus), we will be saved (Romans 10:9). Right there in the car by the side of the road, I was "born of God" and a second birth (spiritual) took place (I John 5:11-12). This birth is clearly stated in John 3:8, "The wind bloweth where it listeth, and thou hearest the sound thereof, but cannot tell whence it cometh, and whither it goeth: so is everyone that is born of the Spirit." The wind, which is the same word used for Spirit, cannot be seen or explained. The word can only be heard or observed in relation to its effect. The new birth is spiritual and invisible. One can only observe the results. It's a decision of faith based upon facts. The first element in trusting Jesus is total dependency.

"And I will give you rest... ye shall find rest unto your souls" are powerful words. It's not only a dependent heart that is necessary but the discovery of divine truth found in Jesus Christ who provides the rest for our souls. Liberation is given through Jesus. We can entrust our spirit, soul and body to Jesus because of who He is. In the Gospel of John, Jesus is revealed as the eternal, pre-existing Son of God, who became man in order to reveal the Father and bring eternal life through his death and resurrection. John says: "Now Jesus did many other signs in the presence of His disciples, which are not written in this book; but these are written that you may believe that Jesus is the Christ, the Son of God, and that believing you may have life in His name" (John 20:30-31).

Jesus is God. "In the beginning was the Word, and the Word was with God, and the Word was God. He was in the beginning with God." In John 1:14 it says that "the Word became flesh." The key term, Word, refers to Jesus. Jesus is fully God. These phrases are vital to understand. "In the beginning"

17

refers to eternity past. It goes beyond his earthly life, beyond even the beginning of creation into eternity. "With God" refers to an affirmation of Christ's separate personality. There is diversity within the Godhead. "And God was the Word" refers to the fact that Jesus is fully divine in all respects. We can trust Jesus because He is God. He has the authority and power to redeem us and bring us into his family.

"Take my yoke upon you and learn of me; for I am meek and lowly in heart" are words of challenge and life-changing possibilities. We must turn around in our thinking. We must turn to Jesus and repent. Our way to acceptance and forgiveness is not acceptable. A complete turnaround and a full change of direction are necessary. We have come to the end of our resources. As we learn of Him, we discover our self-regulations. Work-based convictions will not be sufficient. He is gentle and tender and is calling us to Himself. As we turn from our sin and replace it with faith, a new direction takes place. This is not an intellectual exercise but a whole heart change.

"For my yoke is easy and my burden is light" are words that remind us that salvation in Jesus Christ includes an invitation to surrender. If we want His saving rest, we must take His yoke. The yoke is a symbol of submission. It is used by the master to direct us. Discipline is a natural result of all the elements that are a part of genuine conversion. The yoke is submission to Christ and is not grievous. It is joyous.

My childhood song to live by tells it all, "I have been chosen by the Father, purchased by the Son, and sealed by the Spirit, I'm His Very Own" (Ephesians 1). As a child, I did not understand everything and I do not even now. His grace is amazing and His sovereignty is above us. All He wants me to do is take him at His word. He said, "By one man (Adam), sin entered into the world and death by sin, and so death passed upon all men for all have sinned" (Romans 5:12). "Behold I was shaped in iniquity" (Psalm 51:5). I do not like reading these words but God said it and I have to accept it. I have discovered that "Ye have chosen me" (John 15:16). "It is God who worketh in you both to will and to do of His good pleasure" (Philippians 2:13). He is drawing me to Himself (John 6:44). He has saved me and called me according to His own purpose and grace (II Timothy 1:9).

I am so glad that I was taught by my parents in the early years that "God commendeth His love toward us in that, while we were yet sinners, Christ died for us" (Romans 5:8). As I have grown in Jesus Christ, I have seen His sovereign grace at work. He saved me not by works of righteousness that I have done but according to His mercy by the working of regeneration and renewing of the Holy Spirit (Titus 3:5). I live every day knowing in whom I have believed and am persuaded that He is able to keep that which I have committed unto Him against that day (II Timothy 1:12). Salvation is of the Lord. I am safe because the Father has chosen me, the Son has purchased me and the Holy Spirit has sealed me. Salvation occurs when God changes the heart and unbelievers turn from sin to Christ (Colossians 1:13). Faith is the process for Jesus to enter the heart and dwell there (Ephesians 3:17). Praise the Lord!

THREE

GREAT IS THY FAITHFULNESS
Psalm 23:1-6

The songwriter has written "Great is Thy Faithfulness, O God, my Father; there is no shadow of turning with Thee. Thou changest not; Thy compassions they fail not. As Thou has been Thou forever wilt be." In my childhood, I began singing praises to Jesus Christ. The Bible says in Psalms 57:911 "I will praise you, O Lord, among the nations; I will sing of you among the people. For great is your love, reaching to the heavens; your faithfulness reaches to the skies. Be exalted, O God, above the heavens; let your glory be over all the earth."

There was a real need to add space to our home. The new addition was built as one big room.

It had a big window overlooking the front yard. In those days it seemed to be a large room. It was called our family music room. You could tell why in one glance. You would see a piano, marimba, vibraharp, trumpet, trombone and others. It became our play room and rehearsal space.

During our elementary years, the newspapers would pick up the information about the "triplets" performing. We were the first set of triplets ever to attend Palmer Grade School. It was an attention-getter: "Triple Time Threesome" will play at school carnival. In the Sunday Press, you might read "Triplets sing at Sunday Service." Both of our parents and older sister were active musicians. They were always ready to provide specials for just about any activity if it would glorify our Lord and Savior Jesus Christ.

As a little child, I found a tract entitled "The Lord is My Shepherd" based on Psalms 23:1-6. It became my first sermon, shared with animals and people. This Psalm has become a picture of my first ten years of living. My life has been rooted in God's great faithfulness. Without Psalm 22, there would be no Psalm 23. He who doesn't believe that Christ died for our sins has no claim on the comfort of the risen Savior. In the previous chapter, I shared how and when I made a confession of faith (Romans 10:9,10), "He came to seek and save that which were lost" (Isa.53:6). By accepting Jesus, he produced power and authority in my life. The relationship that was started in those days has continued through the years. I learned to let God be God in my thinking. Today I have to go back to my childhood thinking. As adults we try to fit him into our narrow small view. We must let him lead. He will meet every need. He is "Lord" and Master. He is my Shepherd, boss and caregiver. Music has provided the means for me to fulfill my passion of proclaiming His Word.

Those early years had some uncertainties in them. The World War was in process and the unexpected birth of three babies instead of one baby brought questions like how will God's unlimited resources provide our ever-increasing needs? When you work together and rely on God's promise "I shall not want," you are able to see things happen. Grandpa helped with the numerous diapers that needed washing and grandma helped with feeding the babies along with sister, Mary Lee. She was only three years older but was smart and quite able to help mother. Mother would do what mothers do and dad would spend many hard working hours to provide for us. If you would have asked them about it all, they would have said it was worth it all. They had received from God a special unexpected gift - triplets. God's love can never be diminished. He comes and watches over us. We learned in our childhood that "faith" should say, "I cannot want." He is almighty, all wise, all loving and never changing.

We made it through the birth years but both of my triplet sisters had health difficulties that caused a watchful eye. Ruth was the smallest at 2½ lbs and couldn't keep food down and Evelyn had kidney problems and was also very small. I didn't have any problems. I probably took all the nourishment that was provided when we were in residence in mother.

After two or three years, a special elite medical team came to observe us. Multiple births were still quite a mystery and a marvel. The dignitaries would study our behaviors, skills, abilities and, I suppose, abnormalities. We surprised them after mother had dressed us with the best we had and laid out toys to play with; the trio was all ready for the visitors, mother thought. We didn't want to play with the toys and going outdoors seemed to be a better idea. As a matter of fact, going to the fresh cultivated garden would be just fine. We completed our task by lining up a dozen worms on the front steps of the house. Instead of white garments, they were black with dirt. What a mess to observe. The doctors came to the porch and mother was sad. She asked us why we did what we did. We all responded with positive words, "we dug up worms and placed them in order on the porch so dad could go fishing." I never did find out what happened to the doctors' report. All I know is that through God's faithfulness, he provided good health and necessary needs to keep our household together.

I remember having several accidents that reminded me of God's faithfulness. I ran into a corner of a cedar chest and cut my forehead. Blood was flowing all over my face. The cut was deep but mother pulled the skin together and taped it up. I could have gouged my eye out but God was faithful to spare that. Later, I fell on the ice and my head crashed on the ice. Unfortunately, my eye came in contact with a protruding piece of ice. I spent a lot of time praying and my parents did as well to save my eye. It was a scary experience but I had a lot of help at school with friends. The accident did create some damage, but God was faithful. The next accident was a foolish mistake. I'm grateful that a guardian angel was looking out for me. I had a gun blow up in my hand. The bullet hit the wall and just missed my head. I couldn't hear for several hours, but my head was in one piece and there were no additional holes in my hand. The last accident I had at this point of my life was with a car. In the Psalms we read, "He maketh me to lie down in green pastures", which is a beautiful picture of a flock of sheep grazing in a pasture. I remember running to school because I was late. I wasn't running because I love school so much, but I didn't want to be late. I took a short cut that proved to be a serious mistake. I came head-on with a car as I turned the corner. The driver didn't see me and I didn't see the car coming due to the turn in the road. I tried to get out of the way but the gravel under my feet made me fall. The person in the car slammed on his brakes. The front wheels of the car came to a screeching stop right next to my lower back. It wasn't on a green pasture nor beside quiet waters.

It was on a gravel alley road with a car just about on top of me. I'm glad that I had submitted my life to the Shepherd and that I had pursued and assimilated his Word into my daily life because I know if that car had rolled over me, I would still have had His peace and He would still lead me. In His time, He provides the pasture, quiet water and leadership. He can turn a tragedy into triumph.

There was a time in my childhood that I needed encouragement and restoration. The situation would follow me into my teens and secondary education. My path was straight from a spiritual point of view. This wasn't a spiritual problem. I was in fellowship with Jesus. I found myself in a speech therapy session in grade school. When I first started to talk I had my own means of communication. There were certain words I couldn't say. I was put in a spot many times when teachers, friends or students would just simply laugh at me because the words came out wrong. I don't think the 'enemies' to my sensitivity were trying to be hurtful. They didn't know how to react. Certain words would be said many times over and over in front of me with the expectation that I would be able to repeat them. This became a deep hardship because I couldn't say them, no matter how much kindness or anxiety was put into the effort. This developed into what I call "alternative syndrome." When I couldn't say a certain word, I would substitute it with another. This worked out quite well for me, but it led into other things. When certain subjects became very difficult, I would choose alternatives. My lifestyle was ready to change for substitutes at any given moment. Sometimes it's good to change and have proper substitutes, and at other times it's better to work through the issue and make the best of it. There are certain things we can do and there are other things that others will have to do. I think during this part of history in my life, I can say that the "good shepherd restoreth my soul." I finally was able with His strength to turn around in my thinking. The path for me to follow was found. He will be my guide and comforter.

As a child and young teenager, we would spend part of our summers at a Bible conference. This was always a great time because we would experience top Christian musicians and preachers of the day. As a matter of fact, I started my Biblical resource file in my teens with what I heard in those sessions. I have thousands of topics by reliable people at my fingertips. Of course today, it would be nice to have all that information on CD's. In the early years, I would sit on the first chair of the second row in the auditorium. Those preachers became my heroes.

"He leadeth me in the paths of righteousness." I discovered that the Shepherd could meet all my directional needs. We cannot be independent of God. He guides us. I listened during the sessions, I read the speakers books, I observed their behavior and I, even at times, asked questions. It was a time of preparation. It was a time of learning. It was a time to set goals and objectives for the present and the future. I continue to reflect upon those days today.

My first experience witnessing death came when I was a child. I spent a lot of time with my Grandpa Holmes because we lived in the same house. He was a hard worker. He taught me how to swim and he liked sports. He had a stroke that paralyzed his lower left side and upper right side and his last seven years were spent in a bed. We talked about everything. We listened to the radio together and had our special programs. He was a gentle man and liked having me around. The Bible says, "Yea though I walk through

29

the valley of the shadow of death I will fear no evil." His death didn't take us by surprise. He was ready to meet his Maker. Passing out of this life is an exit out of one life and entrance into another. In death, trials and afflictions, I will trust and not be afraid. I learned that as we enter into the valley, we look for the opening of the gates of glory and Jesus' presence. The shadows in life will come but we don't have to be afraid. His rod protects us and His staff will pull us back into the fold. Our emotional needs can be sound and solid even with bad circumstances in our presence. I felt bad and missed my grandfather but, in my childlike faith, I knew the destiny of spirit, soul and body.

The next phrase in our text, "Thou dost prepare a table before me in the presence of my enemies; thou has anointed my head with oil, my cup overflows." This tells me that God takes care of his sheep. He will provide for our physical needs. The grain and water will provide strength for the sheep and the oil will heal the wounds and hurts. He cares for our needs. The table is a table of victory as the enemy looks on.

It's unfortunate as you read this that you cannot see my mother's face when we helped bring a big St.

Bernard into our small side porch. It took my sisters, some friends and me to help bring that poor creature into our porch. Of course you know that wherever the triplets traveled, the count of individuals would probably increase at least double. The dog had a nail in its foot. We found him in the school playground. We had to help him. We said a little prayer and pulled the nail out of his foot. It wasn't as bad as we thought. Then mother helped put some ointment on it. We couldn't keep the dog but did find his parents. We already had a dog that was my buddy and protector from my sisters. We slept together, ate together, played together and did a lot together. My sisters and I became the animal lovers of the neighborhood. If anyone found a hurt creature, we would be called upon to help. If there was a dead animal, we would be called on to help. We would plan a regular service for that animal and I would share from the tract that I had found. The Psalms would be read and a few comforting memories would be shared. It all became a real ritual. We truly believed that God created and loved the animals and us. I think it became a testimony for all that participated. At lcast, the truth of creation, life, death and compassion would be revealed.

As I leave this period of my life, I am confident when I say "Great is Thy Faithfulness." There are many unsaid words that would cover many pages that I could have shared. When he says, "Surely goodness and mercy shall follow me all the days of my life: and I will dwell in the house of the Lord forever," these words bring encouragement, exhortation and excitement to my entire life. Just think of it, the Word surely brings authority and confidence in what will happen. Goodness and mercy will not simply follow, but will pursue me. In good days and bad days, God will be actively involved with me. I'm thankful that this text was found in my childhood. As a child of God who walks in the path of the Good Shepherd, I am always at home with God. The Shepherd says "I will never leave thee, nor forsake thee." The Lord is my Shepherd and is faithful. Eternity is welcomed with His presence, and daily life is without want.

FOUR

I'D RATHER HAVE JESUS
Exodus 20:3-17

The songwriter has written, "I'd rather have Jesus than silver or gold: I'd rather be His than have riches untold; I'd rather have Jesus than houses or lands, I'd rather be led by His nail-pierced hands. I'd rather have Jesus than anything this world affords today." As I have traveled to many churches, this song has become a favorite to sing. I always played or sang a medley of songs including narration. I heard this song for the first time at a Billy Graham Crusade with Bev Shea singing. I appreciated his sincerity and the deep quality of his voice. The words and melody would follow me, lead me and give me motivation.

In 1952, I graduated from grade school with my

sisters. We were kept together in those years. The teachers said to not divide the triplets; they need to stay together. Academically, we should have been divided but emotionally we were kept together. Today there are many integrated programs for learning. Special tutoring on slow subjects would have been helpful to me. With my speech difficulties and the mastering of the alternative style of thinking, those helpful aids would have been good for me. In the early years, we missed learning words with phonics. I remember memorizing words like cat and dog by pictures not by sounds. In high school, I managed to slide by, but in college I had to do 'double duty' to keep with the flow of things.

As we grew, we continued to perform following the routine in grade school. The sounds of music rehearsal for festivals, parties, and church socials were always coming from the music room. My parents began participating with the American Sunday School Union. This brought a new dimension to our musical ministry and mother story telling. Dad, of course, always played his trombone. He actually played that instrument up to his last breath of air. He died after playing in a band performance.

In those early teen years, we continued to go to the Bible Conference. We would always find some time to retreat to that place. My best friend would travel with me no matter where I would go. His name was Prince. He was a mixed collie-shepherd dog. We spent a lot of time together. He kept me safe from my sisters. My mother loved animals but my dad didn't appreciate them too much. I became concerned for my dog so I made him eat a piece of meat with the Bible text of John 3:16 in it. He certainly had a personality but not a spirit. I was alright with that as long as I knew God created him and loved and cared for all the creatures on the earth. I taught Prince some tricks and he became a real companion. He developed a tumor in his neck and we had to put him to sleep. I have tried to block that experience out of my mind because of certain events that took place. I will leave those details out of this adventure.

In my childhood and early teens, I learned to play the cornet and trombone. My parents and school personnel were my teachers. When I became old enough to travel on the bus across the city, I started instruction at the Christian Music Center. John Scripps was an accomplished trumpeter and owned the center. In those days, it was located on top of a drug store. Today, it is a leading music instrument business in the city. In high school, I enjoyed playing in the band, orchestra, pep band and small ensembles. I also belonged to the drama club and acted in several plays and musical productions. I was never any good at sports but I still tried to participate; I played Saturday basketball. I tried out for the football team. After I got my equipment and the first practice, I threw up and got sick and dropped out. I did receive a letter for being on the track team. I can say truthfully that I never came in first, but I never came in last either.

My greatest involvement was the Campus Life Club. It was originally called Youth for Christ. It met early Friday mornings before school. I grew personally each year in that experience by taking on various responsibilities. I started as a song leader, then vice president and then president. The club was large and at times we had over one hundred in attendance. We were always the leading contender for the city-wide rallies on Saturdays. There was a lot of competition between city clubs. I formed a 'Teen Age Gospel Team' to share the gospel at the other schools and became its director and speaker. At the city-wide events, our club was always prepared and active. I was honored several times and appreciated the opportunity to glorify the Lord.

At sixteen, I began my triple torch career. I began tutoring in my home studio. I preached with my gospel team and I mentored my students. The triple torch would be kept alive for fifty years. At the same time, I developed in my leadership. I became vice president and president of our youth ministry at church. I participated in the church choir and orchestra. From a personal point of view, I have had many friends through the Bible Club at school and church. People would talk to me in the hall way at school that I didn't really know. I was friendly and outgoing but even at the same time I was quiet and sensitive. I had my first real girlfriend at that time. We enjoyed each other and had a lot of fun together. I discovered what that first experience would be to really care for someone of the opposite sex. It was a good journey to real love.

Every four years, the local newspaper seemed to pick up highlights in our lives. It said "Triplets 17 on the 17th in 57." Our teen years were filled with activity. In those years, I never doubted God or His Word. We lived by His rules, or better said, His principles and precepts. The Ten Commandments were committed to memory and observed. Our relationship to God and community was important. If my eyes were taken off of Jesus and my submission to him, I would fail. Through God's grace, when I made mistakes I would be forgiven. The law gives us a picture of where we are and where we should go. Later in my adult years, I would put those thoughts on paper. Read and study *The Ten Commandments for my Life* and you will find them useful.

The laws are grouped into two broad categories: Man's relationship to God and his relationship to the community. "The Book of the Covenant" (Exodus 24:7) was received by Moses on Mount Sinai, orally presented, then written down and read to the people. As a teenager, I have tried to practice them. They have become the foundation of and have brought order to my life. I shall have God before me. My top focus will always be God and his will as it is recorded in his Word. I shall have a spiritual resolve for my personal life. My top focus will be to worship God in spirit and truth, refusing idolatry. I shall have respect for God's name. My top focus will be to have reverence for his name. I shall have a physical and spiritual renewal in my life. My top focus will be complete trust in him in submissive labor. I shall have good family relationships. My top focus will be to magnify in my life what I believe. I shall have value for human life. My top focus will be to minister, protect, preserve and heal. I shall have purity in my life. My top focus will be a lifelong relationship of commitment and trust with a pure heart. I shall have good stewardship in all my activities. My top focus will be placed on honesty regarding God, family and employment relationships. I shall have absolute truth in all my decisions. My top focus will be sincerity in absorbing the truth.

I shall have a covetous heart toward God. My top focus will be an attitude of surrender to God which will provide peace and contentment. I like the word "shall" because it means with determination. It is not just an obligation. It is a necessity. My will has chosen to abide in the law. It is through God's grace and Jesus Christ's accomplishment that I can pursue it. This becomes reality through the Holy Spirit's work in me when I let him work. My mother would remind us that we live in a glass house and you can see through the glass. The law reminds me what I should do and God's gracious spirit provides the enablement. My motivation during those years would be that I'd rather have Jesus than anything. I am thankful for the conscious awareness of the Holy Spirit. I have made many mistakes but he has always brought me back on the straight road.

In 1958, I graduated from High School. The newspaper would once again share the news "Graduation with a Ring to it." We were the first set of triplets to graduate from our grade school and the second set to graduate from High School. This was a special time because we graduated together even though we had different curriculums in school. It was also special because our older sister would graduate from the Grand Rapids Baptist College three-year program at the same time.

FIVE

HOW GREAT THOU ART
Job 23:12

The songwriter has written, "O Lord my God, when I in awesome wonder, consider all the mighty works Thy hands hath made, I see the stars, I hear the rolling thunder; Thy power throughout the universe displayed. How Great Thou Art." My studies have been a life long journey. They include thirty years divided into three sections. Each decade would bring with it a certain unrest, challenge, and adventure along with cultural, social, political, educational and religious issues. It would depend upon the situation of the day. The studies would depend upon the need of the hour. I pursued various disciplines to achieve competence in whatever I was doing to succeed in my triple career. I really never tried to go in three's for everything. It all just came without trying. The triple urge was just simply pushing me forward. In everything, God's awesomeness never decreased. It seemed to be at every turn.

The first decade kept me busy with tutoring at several music stores in every corner of the city. This made tutoring accessible to everyone. I continued the "Teen Age Gospel Team" and preached at mission churches and also was a mentor to my students. During this time, the Word of God continued to be my foundation. The 1960's took me into traditional and non-traditional curriculum. "I have treasured the Word of God" (Job 23:12). It is my fuel to live by. It is a perfect book because it comes from God. I discovered "The fear of the Lord is the beginning of wisdom and the knowledge of the Holy One is understanding" (Prov. 9:10). The supernatural one "The Great I Am" (Ex. 3:13-14) is self-existent, self-sufficient and eternal. I have spent time at Moody Bible Institute, Grand Rapids School of Bible and Music and the National Bible College. Some of my studies were in residence and others were through correspondence. The goal was to complete a major in Biblical Studies and earn a Bachelor of Theology degree (BTh) in order to be licensed and ordained into the Gospel ministry. This would give me doctrinal understanding of the many church schools I would be consulting at. It would also prepare me for pastoral interest. I became convinced over and over again that the Bible I learned about in my childhood was genuine. It is perfect in origin (II Tim. 3:16-17). It is God breathed. It is the very Word of God not limited to human limitations. It was "produced by the Holy Ghost" (II Pet. 1:21). The Divine Genius carried it along. He moved upon, in and through human authors. The translations of God's thoughts and will to humanity is through language and inspiration. We are not permitted to judge the Bible by our experience but we must judge our experience by the Bible, the sure word (II Pet. 1:19).

My daily activities would prove to be steady and uncertain at times but "His words shall not pass away" (Matt. 24:35). They would be perfect in purpose penetrating my very spirit and soul (Heb. 4:12-13). When I would take heed, they would provide discernment and wisdom for every decision (John 14:17). He resides in us and develops wisdom. He is the very breath of air. He provides the Scripture (Eph 6:17), "The sword of the spirit which is the Word of God." All we have to do is "hide it in our hearts" and act on it (Ps. 119:11). I learned how to study. I enjoyed research. I discovered where to go and how to accomplish my goals. This decade of education became a tool to prepare me for more in-depth studies. The new curriculum I would pursue would be built upon the original courses. At the same time I moved from tutoring to Department Manager at Grinnell Brothers Music Company. Later I would be asked to join the Marshall Music Company, the state's largest music distributor of Band and Orchestra instruments, as a school representative and new school coordinator. I would also manage my own consulting service.

The 1970's challenged me for further studies. I accepted my first interim pastorate. I learned early that people are hard to work with. My boss, Jesus, was great. I've never found any fault with him. He has never failed me. He is sovereign: "The earth is the Lord's and all it contains, the world and those who dwell in it" (Ps. 24:1). He was the founder of it. He created it. He has established it and He has sustained it. What God's soul desires, he does (Job 23:13). He works all things after His will (Eph. 1:11). The Lord has made everything for its own purpose, even the wicked for the day of evil (Prov. 16:4). "Our God in the heavens, He does whatsoever He plans" (Ps. 115:3). In Psalm 19:6 it says "the Lord our God the Almighty reigns." His attributes guarantee his sovereignty. There's nothing he cannot do. There is nothing he does not know and no location he does not exist. I learned that He knows what I'm facing. He says that He'll face it with you, and He can do the job. I'm learning to say "Thy will be done" because God rules absolutely over the affairs of men. There are no accidents with God. He does whatsoever He chooses. As we live in the world, we must think like God does, "God allows us to make choices. The destinations have been made but the route is affected by our choice. God is going to get there whether through us, around us, over us, by us or in spite of us." I loved preparing sermons. I became a master at programming. I needed to learn some more about how people think. Don't misunderstand, I love people. I know the Bible but I needed to understand how the head and heart work. In the second decade,

I learned that we should obtain as much knowledge as possible. We will still come up short.

After several years, I returned back to Grand Rapids. At this time I was married and had a son. Continuing education was difficult in relationship to time spent at home, work, school and study. Sometimes I would forget sleep time or fun time. Joy, my wife, was a great helpmate. Her skills in typing and making sense out of all my research papers helped me to succeed. She is also an accomplished pianist. Therefore, she accompanied me at recitals and music juror examinations. I received a sizable grant from Aquinas College. As long as I kept up the grades, I could continue with the grant. The Lord helped me do just that. Of course, I liked what I was studying. I even wrote some of my own curriculum. I received credit for English because I wrote a booklet for publication entitled "The Gospels". I became minister of music at two churches during this period of my life. They both became a place for the display of my conducting skills and the accomplishment of certain academic requirements for conducting. I was honored to conduct several community-wide musicals. During this time I was teaching, preaching and mentoring. I don't really know how I was able to keep it all together. I graduated from John Wesley College with a Bachelors of Arts degree (BA). It was very broad in liberal arts equipping me with the triple major in Religion/Bible, Music Education and Social Science. After additional studies in education and psychology at Nazareth College, a teaching institution, I was recommended for teaching certification.

I learned a lot about humanity; the biological, psychological and even spiritual aspects. I was renewed in my thinking that "No prophetic scripture can be explained by one's unaided mental powers" (II Peter 1:20). The spiritual origin of the Word necessitates spiritual understanding. A natural man cannot receive spiritual truth. The whole concept of 'Scriptural meaning' indicates that the ministries of the New Testament are "not of the letter, but of the spirit, for the letter killeth but the spirit giveth life (2 Cor. 3:6). It is the spirit that beareth witness, because the spirit is truth (I John 5:6). We can't intellectualize or bargain with God, rather by faith we understand. My first decade of studies (1960's) paved the way and gave foundation to the second decade (1970's). Not everything you learn takes permanent root; we do not have enough soil to grow that much produce, and not all the seeds that fall into your learning tray are worthy of being cultivated. I was able to accomplish my goal once again with God's help.

In the 1980's, I found myself already with a healthy habit of studying. It seemed that everywhere I traveled in life's journey I would continue in my lifelong learning process. My interest in education wouldn't be completed with BTh and BA degrees. I became a Senior Pastor of a church on Torch Lake with interest in theology, education and counseling. In this third decade, alternative, extensive and distant education became very useful for a full time busy professional person. I naturally fell into pursuing a Master of Art and Doctor of Philosophy curriculum. My church became a part of the graduate curriculum. I enjoyed independent research; after my previous years of experience, I became proficient at this method of study. Everything I did at the church became a part of my graduate field project. It was entitled "The Development of a Local Assembly." After three years of intensive course-taking and field project innovations, I was ready to defend my Biblical Christianity Applied Project. It was a great opportunity to share Biblical truth to a liberal team of examiners. The oral exam was based on scholarship and how I presented my project. It was similar to my ordination years before, except that the first examination was given by a group of ministers upon the authority of the church and the second was composed of friendly but anti-Christian professors. The Holy Spirit led in everything I said. I had confidence and boldness. I was declared a graduate with distinction. I can truthfully say, "Hold to the things that you have learned" (II Tim. 3:12-14). The foundation and solid ground is the Holy Scripture. Anyone can read the Bible, but without the Holy Spirit's guided intelligence, the information is worth little. All of my prior training in Bible College and Liberal Arts College paid off. The study of the Word of God applied to other disciplines brought confidence. The graduate-planned program was offered in the British style of independent studies. I completed the curriculum and oral examination for my doctoral field project which displayed careful scholarship and satisfactory development of pastoral skills. I was awarded the PhD degree in religion with a specialty in Biblical Christianity through the graduate school of Columbia Pacific University.

I have a broad and integrated awareness of my overall field (Bachelor's level), and a specific developed area of competence and skills (Master's level). Now I am a teacher/innovator and a creative thinker in my specialty (Doctoral level). I was designated as an international mentor in religion upon graduation. This would give me an opportunity to serve graduate students in several countries.

"How Great Thou Art" will ring in my ears as I worship Him and serve Him. My only real goal from day one was to be "approved unto God" (II Tim. 2:15). The study of the Holy Scripture is the way to satisfy God. I have learned to cut the Scriptures straight and have become adequately equipped for all good works. I have discerned that "the entrance of thy Words giveth light" (Psalm 119:30). The Bible shows us to ourselves as God-created beings. It reveals that we come from God's hand with a purpose and plan, and that sin has entered and perverted the entire race. By one man, sin entered into the world, and death by sin (Romans 5:12). The only way to believe and be convinced of the "sure word" is through coming to the way, the truth and life found in Jesus (John 14:6). My passion is to proclaim Him in all things.

The great aim of the Christian life is not simply to know a set of ethics, but that "I may know Him" (Phil. 3:10). Throughout this whole chapter, I have emphasized why I believe in the "sure word", the Holy Scripture. It has led me all the way. When we miss Jesus, we miss what God wanted us to know. Through believing in, being cleansed by, trusting in and relying upon Him, we have life. This proclamation will continue in my life. Many people think of themselves as Christians. They are part of a community, a culture, a home and an organization which is Christian in concept and character. They are Christianized but they are not vitally related to Jesus Christ. All my studies have brought me to a relationship in knowing Jesus. I am grateful that I can sing "How Great Thou Art."

SIX

STANDING ON THE PROMISES
2 Peter 1:19

The songwriter has written, "Standing on the promises that cannot fail, when the howling storms of doubt and fear assail, by the living Word of God I shall prevail. I'm standing on the promises of God." I live in the 'now.' I can make daily decisions through an eternal heavenly-directive way because I am encircled with God's promises. Being 'still' has started the path. Simplicity and silence will drown out the noise and lead me to God's presence. I intend to hear His voice through His Word. The Holy Spirit dwelling within makes the abundant life a reality, not merely a possibility. The ability to put faith, hope and love into action began through His Word. His Word has opened up the door to interaction. Communication with God has brought dependence and reliance. This has been demonstrated through the re-education process and behavioral change. My life's routine has centered around His promises. This will cause radical living and bring with it ridicule, but rewards will be given at the end of it all.

As I delight in his law (Scripture), I will be blessed. The promise, "Blessed is the man who walketh not in the council of the ungodly...but his delight is in the law of the Lord" has laid the foundation (Psalm 1:12). I grew up believing in the Bible. I am extremely glad that I can say that. I do not take it for granted. I have had to unlearn a few things but the primary fundamental doctrines have been planted well into my brain waves. In those early days, if someone asked me to walk across the lake, I would have believed that God could accomplish it. If you asked why I believe, the answer would simply be that someone did it in Scripture. As long as they had their eyes on Jesus, no sinking took place. This belief remains secure because my spirit, soul and body have been entrusted in faith to Jesus Christ. I have become a soldier of Jesus Christ because "Jesus loves me this I know, for the Bible tells me so."

I can rely on the promise "Blessed is the man who walketh not in the council of the ungodly...but his delight is in the law of the Lord" because the Bible is dependable. I love books. They are my tools. I use them for many different reasons. Recently, I laid an old family Bible on a stand in my study to remind me of my history as well as the Scriptures. It is a precious book to have. It was passed down to me through my grandmother (Grandma Holmes) and to her though her grandparents. It was entered according to an Act of Congress in the year 1892 in the Office of the Librarian of Congress at Washington.

Everyone has to make a decision about the Bible, "the sure word" (2 Peter 1:19). There is no escape. Either you may cherish, read, ignore, respect, dissect, study or hate it, but a decision has to be made. I began to read that old family Bible and reflected on the fact that even though the original was written centuries ago, it is pertinent for me today. The Bible repeatedly speaks in terms that involve all generations. Jesus claimed, "Heaven and earth will pass away, but my words shall not pass away" (Matthew 24:35). The prophet Isaiah said, "The grass withers, the flowers fade, but the word of our God stands forever" (Isaiah 40:8). It claims within itself to come from an all-knowing, all-powerful, personal and exclusively-existing God. You can laugh at the Bible, and you can think that it is not relevant today. You can be a skeptic, religionist, agnostic, atheist, Satanist or just a naïve person with good ethical standards, but the Bible is still for you.

As I was reading that old family Bible, I couldn't help realize the uniqueness of it. It is different, it is one of a kind, it has no equal, it is a book written over a 1,500 year span and it was written over 40 generations. It was written by more than 40 authors from every walk of life including kings, peasants, philosophers, fishermen, poets, statesmen, scholars, etc. It was written in three continents; Asia, Africa and Europe. It was written in three languages; Hebrew, Aramaic and Greek. It covers hundreds of topics. Yet, the biblical authors spoke with harmony and continuity from Genesis to Revelation. There is one unfolding story: God's redemption of man.

There are many reasons why the Bible is important to apply to one's life. Its dependability is connected to its uniqueness, made up of the canon, bibliographical test, internal evidence, prophesies fulfilled, historical geography, archeological evidences, miracles and its transforming power. Jesus Christ has made a direct challenge to my will to trust Him. He says, "I have been standing at the door and I am constantly knocking. If anyone hears me calling him and opens the door, I will come in" (Revelation 3:20). I discovered that when I accepted Jesus Christ as my Savior and believed He died on the cross for me and that He was resurrected, through faith my life has been changed from the inside out. I am convinced that the Bible is dependable because of the divine genius who has put it together and it has fulfilled the promise of blessing.

Holy men from God spoke as they were carried along by the Holy Spirit (2 Peter 1:21). The genius of this record is through the Holy Spirit moving upon, in and through human authors. The translation of God's thoughts and will to humanity is through language and inspiration (carried along by the Holy Spirit). The Bible (66 books contained in the Old and New Testaments) has had a divine intervention. "No prophecy ever resulted from human design." (2 Peter 1:21). "We have a more sure word of prophecy" (2 Peter 1:19) in the Bible. We are not permitted to judge the Bible by our experiences but we must judge our experience by the Bible, "the sure word."

I am convinced that the Bible is dependable because of my spiritual understanding. In my life and others' lives, Scripture has fulfilled the promise of blessing.

"No prophetic scripture can be explained by one's unaided mental powers" (2 Peter 1:20). The spiritual origin of the word necessitates spiritual understanding. Natural men cannot receive spiritual truth. The whole concept of scriptural ministry indicates that the minister of the New Testament is "not of the letter, but of the spirit, for the letter killeth but the spirit giveth life" (2 Corinthians 3:6). "It is the spirit that beareth witness, because the Spirit is truth" (I John 5:6). I can't intellectualize or bargain with God; by faith I understand. The foundation and solid ground are the Holy Scriptures. Anyone can read the Bible, but without the Holy Spirit's guided intelligence the information is worth little. The study of the Word of God brings confidence. I am convinced that the Bible is dependable because of my relationship with Jesus Christ and it has fulfilled the promises of blessing. "These are written in order that you may believe that Jesus is the Christ, the anointed One, the Son of God. Through believing and cleaving to, and trusting in and relying upon him, you may have life through His name, through what He is" (John 20:31). The life is in Him, 'what He is', and not through any religious duties, however beautifully performed. It is terrifying to know that this plain word, this "testimony of Jesus," can be in a man's possession, and he can miss the God of revelation. When we miss Jesus, we miss what God wants us to know. The great aim of the Christian life is not simply to know a set of ethics, but that "I may know Him" (Philippians 3:10).

"Blessed is the man who walketh not in the council of the ungodly…but his delight is in the law" (Psalm 1:1-2). As a soldier of Jesus Christ, I have been blessed through obeying His Word. The promise has become real in my life. I think everyone will come to a point in their life where they will be convinced that the Bible is either true or it is not. My own mind and heart had to be convinced even though I was trained as a child and young adult. I appreciated my early foundation, but I had to learn, decide and discover my own answers. I was in Chicago taking special studies at the American Conservatory of Music. One evening I picked up a book dealing with many reasons why I shouldn't believe in Christianity and the Bible. I had to come to terms with following the Bible all the way, partially, or not at all. Satan tried to be deceptive in my mind and the council of the ungodly raised some questions. Amazing as it might sound, because I have delighted in the study of God's book, the Bible, it began to convince me. Many scriptures came to my mind when my soul was troubled. Jesus said, "Let not your heart be troubled, ye believe in God, believe also in me…I am the way, the truth and the life" (John 14:1,6). I threw the other book away. It really didn't have solid reasons in it. It just gave testimony of many Christians in the church that have been poor witnesses.

I was walking on the shore of Lake Michigan and looking into the starlit sky above the blue waters. The Holy Spirit had reminded me of the Bible verses that I had learned years ago. The witness of divinity and my own spirit were united. I was truly blessed. The council of the ungodly will lead you astray but His Word will bless your life. I believe in the dependability of the Scriptures. They continue to bless me in so many different ways.

SEVEN

GUIDE ME
Colossians 3:15-18

The songwriter has written, "Guide my steps Lord Jesus and lead me in your way, I want to be like you each moment of the day. Keep me from all sin and cleanse me within. Let God's word be my power; and strengthen me each hour." This is one of the songs I composed. It speaks of my journey in following Jesus. It was written at the dinner table. After talking with the family about Jesus Christ, we all decided to confess our sins to him. We wanted to be released of anything that would stop us from walking with Him. Our desire in the family was to allow His power to lead us and keep us safe. We would follow Colossians 3:16-17, "Let the Word of

Christ dwell in you richly in all wisdom, teaching and admonishing one another in Psalms, hymns and spiritual songs, singing with grace in your hearts to the Lord. And whatsoever ye do in word or deed, do all in the name of the Lord Jesus, giving thanks to God and the Father by Him."

In my life, the proclamation of the Word has found its way primarily through music. All styles have been important to me but sacred theology and sacred music go hand-in-hand. The words, "Let the word of Christ dwell in you" is the beginning of the process. People in the church and not of it would like to minimize God's Word. We can't build our lives with man-made traditions, religious rules, human philosophies or false teachers. When Christ dwells in us, it means that He has transformed us and we have experienced His grace and peace. He feels at home in our hearts. The word 'dwell' means the same as filled according to Ephesians 5:18. As a young man and now a senior citizen, I have carried a little "Pastoral Prescription" pad. I created it to give out to people whom I visit. My first prescription was written for myself. It says, "Above all... Christ" (John 3:31). I needed to be reminded to do some spiritual daily activities. Ask to be filled by the Holy Spirit (Luke 11:13), be fruitful and grow in discipline (I Peter 2:2), confess sinfulness (I John 1:9) and be a witness (Acts 1:8). When I do these activities, I'm all set for the day. If I forget, I'll pay the price. My early music proclamation of the Word was fulfilled through tutoring. At sixteen, I played trumpet with my older sister accompanying me at the piano. Our pastor asked if I would tutor his son so he might someday glorify the Lord in this same way. With the one student came several others. I was able to give up my lawn cutting business. I had a good little business but I was ready for a change.

Tutoring became more than a financial pursuit. I loved to watch the children mature in their musicianship. I had many opportunities one-on-one to share my faith in Jesus Christ. I developed in my skills as well. To be more accessible, I had a studio in every direction in the city. I think I have worked in just about every music store in the city at some time or another in my life.

I remained firm in my Bible foundation. It continued with these words "Richly in all wisdom, teaching." I knew nourishment from God's Word was necessary. It would equip me for every good work (II Timothy 3:16-17). I was devoted to Scripture. My life was maintained through the living Word. I was dependent upon it and therefore it directed my life. I will be tutoring until God calls me home or I don't have the health to pursue it. Tutoring introduced me to all the music stores in town. The largest downtown store at the time invited me to learn the music business. Grinnell Brothers Music Company was a part of the American Music Stores, Inc. I worked in many different departments. I moved up in various positions to department manager and possibly head manager. I enjoyed keeping track of the inventory. I was organized so my job was fun, interesting and educational. I learned about all the major instrument manufacturers. For my own students I would address what instrument was the best for them and their different types of music performance. I learned public relations and how to work with people. I became manager of my own independent music education consultant service. I enjoyed education more than business, even though they were integrated into one enterprise. I started out teaching music at West Side Christian School and finished up at East Side Christian School. I had good relations with my former business associates. I provided instruments to my students through them. Several years later, I was invited by the state's largest music industry, Marshall Music Company, to become a school service representative and new school coordinator.

Over the years, I started fifty school music departments in private and public schools. I never was interested in making money. Business was lucrative because education was the central goal. I remember at one school that I created the need to have instruments. I tested the students, coordinated the teaching staff and provided the financial necessities. They bought $100,000.00 worth of instruments. As I approached the end of my career, I have been a team teacher at several schools. I helped to teach the teacher to teach. I'm not a master teacher, but enjoyed helping others to do a more proficient job. The Lord Jesus Christ was in all that activity and the providence of God was evident.

The Scripture says, "Teach and admonish one another." The word 'admonish' means to excite, advise and exhort. I'm using all these ideas in my performance opportunities. Performing has always been a nervous experience for me but always a fulfilling activity. In my childhood, we shared in many Sunday school events, school and community activities. We added instruments to our program in our early teens and more opportunities would arrive on our door steps like concerts, recitals and festivals. Young adulthood and adulthood would provide conducting experiences. I had the privilege of conducting a city-wide Christian school concert in Grand Rapids. Several hundred vocalists and instrumentalists participated. The only part I didn't like was climbing up onto the podium. It was too high and I have a fear of heights. There was also a time when I was ready to conduct the first beat and the first row of vocalists fainted. I have conducted many church-wide musicals. I think I have enjoyed the conducting more than the instrumental performance. I have formed several ensembles over the years like the Teen Age Gospel Team, The Musical Messengers and the Messengers Inc. They were all exciting adventures. One of the ensembles became the nucleus for a larger group to perform with John Peterson in his premier musicals in Grand Rapids.

This was of course a great thrill. I spent two years traveling for a humanitarian organization in music and speaking. This was an exhaustive time but full of growing opportunities. I learned that my body and mind can appreciate others doing this kind of work but I was not made for it. Physically, I can't do that kind of ministry any longer but my mind remains ready for it.

The Scripture continues, "With psalms and hymns and spiritual songs." I love this verse because one of my most rewarding excitements is putting Scripture and songs together. Those medleys have become expressions of worship. The knowledge of the Bible goes hand-in-hand with worship expression. When we sing a hymn, we address the Lord. When we sing a spiritual song, we address each other. In these last few years, I have written and arranged several medleys. *The Lord's Prayer*, *Heroes of Faith* and *Songs to Live By* have been performed in several school functions.

In all the musical activities I have participated, I have always kept the phrase "sing with grace in your heart to the Lord" in mind. Singing or playing an instrument must be done because we have God's grace in our hearts. Our performance before God is perfect even if we are out of tune. He listens to the heart. It's nice if the intonation is correct. We must do our best but God knows what is best.

The text ends with "Whatsoever you do in word or deed." This refers to all we say and do should be associated with Jesus. Our conduct magnifies our Savior and Lord. I am identified with Jesus. The word 'Christian' is found in the Scripture three times. My philosophy of music and its education is centered on the "Name of Jesus." I am so thankful to God. He has provided everything I need to do to glorify Him. In the process, I was awarded a Distinguished Service Award from the Michigan Association of School Boards for my contribution to education. I was honored on Teacher Appreciation Day from the Holland S.D.A. School. I was privileged to receive the yearbook dedication from Eastside Christian School in Grand Rapids. I was appointed to the professional extension faculty of the Sherwood Music School in Chicago (A College of Music). The most meaningful tribute came from a teenager from the Algoma Christian School. She said, "I have you to thank for my musical theory skills. God has given me a talent that through the years you have picked up on and helped me discover. Thank you so much for obeying and being a humble man of God" (Ashley Marie Lyons).

EIGHT

IN THE SERVICE OF THE KING
Matthew 25:21

The songwriter has written "I am happy in the service of the King, I have peace and joy that nothing else can bring. Every talent I will bring, in the Service of the King." A few years ago someone asked me, why have you followed a triple career? You have been busy in ministry and education and now you include para church leadership to your already too busy schedule. My first answer was that it is hard for me to say no, but then when I see something that needs to be done and I am able to designate and motivate others to help, I just simply fall into the activity. I'm sure my life has been hard to follow at times but as the songwriter has written, "Thro' sunshine and the shadow I can sing, in the service of the King." Back in my young adulthood, John 9:4 impressed upon my heart to "work for the night cometh when no man can work." Now, in my senior adulthood, I can see the truth of that Scripture. The organizational development of several para church leadership opportunities came into place while I was still serving in ministry and education. It seems each activity grew out of the former ministry. They all had to do with John 9:4. We live in a fallen world where good behavior is not always rewarded and bad behavior not always punished. Therefore, innocent people sometimes suffer. If God took suffering away whenever we asked, we would follow him for comfort and convenience not out of love and devotion. Regardless of the reasons for our suffering, Jesus has the power to help us deal with it. Each para church ministry was developed to help a personal need and give strength through the trial and offer a deeper perspective on what is happening.

As I reflected, I discovered that the para church ministries fall into a preparation period, a volunteer period and a professional period. There was a time to be molded and to understand through sensitivity and discernment, a time to add understanding to those lifestyles through involvement and a time to put it all together. Sometimes I like to look at it with the privilege to encourage, exhort and enlighten. I like people and want to serve them.

As a child, I was given little child-like jobs to do. My folks volunteered in helping the American Sunday School Union. We would go to an Hispanic neighborhood and have a Bible class. My mother was a master story teller. We always learned something new in those classes. I would make sure everyone was welcomed. I would pass out chorus sheets and probably select someone to assist me. The color of the skin didn't make any difference to me nor did the language. I made friends with ease. I was quiet but sensitive to the other kids. I would be the first to sit by them. I really wanted them to meet Jesus. We would sing "Jesus loves me, this I know" and I would tell them my favorite Bible verse, John 3:16. A summary of the Bible was shared. I am sure in those days that we did some good. I hope I'll meet some of those children in heaven. When I started to play the trumpet in my tenth year, we would travel to the mission. The Mel Trotter Mission was on Monroe Street at that time. My dad played the trombone.

The two instruments were made for each other. We performed some good duets in praise to our Lord Jesus Christ. I have some of those duets on CD's. Once again, it didn't make any difference who was performing because the testimony was for Jesus.

As a teenager, I was involved with Youth for Christ Clubs. I found myself again witnessing to the loner, outcast, neglected and rejected. It seemed that those people were drawn to me. As president of our high school club, I was always friendly and invited everyone to the club. I think I developed a sensitive nature in my childhood that simply grew with me into my teens. One day I invited a young man home with me whom I met in the school yard. He was tired, dirty, hungry and without a home. My mother fed him and gave him some clothes but all of a sudden we found a gun in his pocket. Now what do we do? We had to go to the authorities. With a lot of praying and maturing, we made it through the ordeal and everything turned out alright. I would do everything over again if I had to do it again. We had a huge club at school which gave me many opportunities to help others.

When I was teaching, I was led to start an

instrumental music department at an inner city school. I had a great time working with dysfunctional and messed up family situations. If I had my way, I would have adopted all of the kids. They had some real talents and abilities. Someday I may go back to the Academy and rekindle the work.

As a young adult, I started teaching at Westside Christian School opposite from the previous school I mentioned. Everything was different. I enjoyed the privilege to teach music as a proclamation of the Word. My band room became a place to jam with students. The Bible became our resource book. Music is a great outlet in becoming friends. Encouragement and exhortation have been combined to assist the students. I have welcomed them to discussion sessions. I was able to integrate Biblical truth into a personal relationship with Jesus Christ. Christianity is progressive. We have to learn to relate everything we do and think through the Scriptures. We had numerous topics to relate to.

I completed the preparation period and began to move into the volunteer period. It started with the immediate needs of our church. We had only a few teenagers so I needed to find some teenagers.

The school is the best place to find them. I was an ordained minister of the gospel but I was also a certified teacher so I became a substitute teacher. Many stories could be shared in relationship to teaching, but I need to keep to the volunteer service. The substituting led into the guidance department. I was given the opportunity to come alongside of many troubled teens. This generated interest in the church. Therefore, I hit two birds with one stone; church growth in the youth department and assistance in the school guidance department. This led into my first elected position as a trustee on the school board. Working with youth brought me in contact with a chronic liar, family abuse situations, school drop-outs and drug addiction. Through God's grace, some of the youth turned to Jesus. This was an exciting time. I have many pleasant memories to reflect upon. The substituting and guidance led into the probation court endeavors. One day I walked into the county court house to support a teenage friend. When his name was called, I walked up in front of the judge with him. The judge thought I was his attorney. As a Pastor, I asked if I could say something on the boy's behalf. The judge let me talk. After I finished, the judge asked me to come to his chambers. I wondered what I did wrong. Am I in trouble? I wondered if I said something to offend him. The judge didn't request my presence but demanded it. I stood before the judge and he put his hand out to shake mine. He said that it was a pleasure to meet me and find someone who was interested enough to stand up for the teenager. He said that if I had time and a place to handle twenty youth, he would be glad to assign them to me. It was a pleasant surprise. During this time I became acquainted with the Baptist Children's Home and Family Ministries. Some other homes were opened up for care in the community as well.

I was in the court house many times. One of those times I met a young attorney. He had just received Jesus Christ in his life. He had never lost a case. He was tough but fair. He was good at doing lawyer work but very poor at personal relationships. He had been married several times and divorced. He needed mentoring so I became his biblical advisor. I assisted him in starting a new ministry in conciliation. The Northern Michigan Conciliation Service was created and established. I was appointed the founding chairman. We worked on building solid relationships with couples on the verge of divorce who needed comfort. If we follow marriage and family relationship concepts in God's Word, we will have the answers needed to be successful. I remember praying for couples right in a corner of the court house seeking a solution. The couples would respond and want to change. Then we had to deal with their counsel representatives. Most of them worked out to the favor of the couple. Meditation seminars were set up to introduce divorce problems to the church. Counseling for the family, marriage and remarriage problems all came into focus.

Let me remind you that during all these para church activities, I was a pastor, educator and graduate student. I learned to apply everything I did to the work at hand. Everything was done in an orderly way and with proficiency. Organizational abilities were a part of my thinking system. I'm grateful for the preparation time during the 1940's and 1950's, the volunteer outreach during the 1960's and 1970's and the professional encounter in the 1980's and 1990's. When I became a Pastor, I always tried to encircle myself with professionals in different disciplines. They would become my resource people.

If I needed help with assurance that I'm doing and saying the right things or to give me confidence or to have someone to discuss deep matters with, they were at my fingertips. I had a theology professor to help with Satanism issues. I had a social worker to help with an overview of social-relational problems. I had an accountant to assist with money matters. I had a psychiatrist to help with mental-medical issues and I had a medical doctor to assist with any physical or internal issues. I could call on these people at any time. They were Christians and loved the Lord. The American Association of Christian Counselors has been an ongoing educational process for me too. My primary resource has been the Bible and the Holy Spirit as my counselor.

I created a pastoral support ministry. It was called the Northwest Antrim County Ministerial Association. We had twenty pastors, representing different denominational backgrounds, meeting monthly. The fellowship was built upon Biblical Christianity concepts. We all believed in Jesus Christ through faith and enjoyed discussion on secondary issues. This gave pastors an opportunity to share church or personal problems and be lifted up through prayer and counsel. I have also had fun in helping to develop a marriage check-up and pre-marital program at Calvary Church in Grand Rapids. This was built on ten sessions leading to marriage vows. Faith and spiritual evaluation, marriage equals oneness, relational survey, couple communication, listening inventory, budget accountability, God's sexuality plan, marriage covenant, any loose ends and commitment. I continue to use this method when asked to counsel pre-marital couples today.

I asked the Lord for a more challenging opportunity to serve and He took me back to the mission. In my childhood, I played special music for the men and women before they had their dinner. You never knew what would happen. Later in Chicago I counseled at the Pacific Garden Mission. This was exciting but also a dangerous experience. I met a lot of strange people but they all needed the Savior just like me. I remember returning from Moody Church at night and two prostitutes tried to pick me up and then someone tried to rob me at knife point. In the 1990's, I was asked to direct the discipleship ministry at the Kalamazoo Gospel Mission. This is an addictive deliverance center. It had an international flavor.

The men represented Europe, West Africa, Trinidad, England, Mexico and our own United States. It was interesting and exciting. I would learn to deal with different cultures in addition to the situations the men were facing. Men in recovery are traveling from helplessness to powerlessness to forgiveness. Liquor will leave you breathless, drugs will leave you senseless, but Jesus Christ won't leave you regardless. This ministry took me into many amazing situations. The Holy Spirit had to be present. My book *Discipling Dynamics* was written at this time. It was a pastoral biblical response to life's daily issues. Every time we had counseling in what I called "talk therapy" sessions, we would place our confidence on God's Word and find an answer. Along with many other strategies, success would be the result. I was pleased and proud of the guys and grateful and thankful to Jesus Christ for the Michigan State Senate Resolution No. 300 given to the mission recognizing its contribution through the Discipleship Program. I was also honored by the Louisiana Baptist University with a Doctor of Ministry degree for integrating Christianity into the organizational development of several pastoral, educational and para church leadership ministries.

NINE

LAMB OF GLORY
Romans 12:1-2

The songwriter has written "Hear the story from God's Word that kings and priests and prophets heard. There would be a sacrifice and blood would flow to pay sin's price. Precious lamb of glory, love's most wondrous story, heart of God's redemption of man – worship the lamb of glory." My passion has always been to proclaim the word of God. The Lord has helped me do it through music education and worship. He has also given me opportunity through para church ministries. Now I have come to the preaching, teaching and pastoral care ministries. I am a minister of the gospel. It is a delight to share the story of Jesus and His sacrifice. He is the precious "lamb of glory." It has been my priority in life to honor and give reverence to Jesus Christ. As I have grown, I understand a little more about what is involved. As I reflect about the pastoral ministries, I have been challenged to think about what I have learned through those years.

Someone asked me, "What is a spiritual Christian?" I think the pastor must be a Biblical spiritual Christian. I use the word Biblical because I base everything I have learned on the authority of the Scriptures. I use the word spiritual because I am thinking on spiritual terms and our dedication to a godly, righteous and holy life. I use the word Christian because Jesus Christ is my Savior, Lord and the head of the church. I will explore Romans 12:1-2 in relation to my church ministries.

Three valuable lessons have been learned that have followed my entire life. I memorized Romans 12:1-2 many years ago. I have been learning new lessons from the text every day since that day. Paul writes the text through the Holy Spirit, the divine genius of the Scripture. The first eleven chapters reveal doctrine. From chapter twelve to the end, it deals with application. I love how the text begins; it gives me encouragement and strength. It says "I beseech you." God is talking to me and telling me that he is my helper and has come along side of me. I am not alone because the "therefore" refers to things that have taken place in my life. The four times "therefore" is in Romans refer to condemnation (3:20), justification (5:1), assurance (8:1) and dedication (12:1). I am a believer. I have been redeemed through the sacrifice of the "Lamb of glory." The penalty of sin has been solved. I'm accepted through Jesus Christ and have the assurance that I am secure in Him. When the Scripture says "brethren," it means that I have a relationship with God. This relationship is based upon Christ's death, resurrection, ascension and Pentecost. This is Biblical Christianity at its core.

I remember back in my teens. Huge decisions were made in those years. Maybe that is the reason that I love working with teenagers. My gospel praise team was ministering at a youth rally. I was speaking and I came to the end of my sermon. The Holy Spirit caused a deep sense of concern and discernment. I was facing a lot of youth my own age that needed to respond to the challenge that was just delivered. I thought about my own soul. I prayed that the convicting power of the Holy Spirit would cause a stir among us.

I also prayed that this occasion might become my call to ministry. I reached into the heavens and asked if my Lord Jesus wanted this young man to minister. If this was so, I asked the Lord to send a great response to the service, not only for confession of faith and dedication decision but to show me His will. At the end of the service, I opened my eyes and twenty youth had responded to the invitation to pray and my answer was nailed in my mind in humble appreciation. It has been many years but it seems like yesterday in my heart and mind. Seven years later, in an itinerate ministry after earning a bachelor's degree in theology, I was licensed and ordained by a Bible-believing church.

I have learned three major lessons in my pastoral ministries. It would take many words to share all the things I have learned during this time. Therefore, I have taken the top three. Everything else builds upon them. Through my life on a daily basis, I have thought about the divine residence in me, the divine transformation taking place in me and the divine will at work in me. After Christ came into my heart through the faith that He gave me, He said, "present"(Romans 12:1,2) your body, mind and will to me. The word 'present' means a definite decision. It's a once-and-for-all commitment. The words "mercies of God and reasonable service" gives me the reasons that are logical for me to give my total life to Him. As I reflect on what He has done for me, giving of Himself and then giving the Holy Spirit to me, how can I not give myself to Him? The Bible says, "present your body a living sacrifice, holy, acceptable." I have to recognize the divine residence in my body. A change has taken place because now I am a new person: "....if any man be in Christ, he is a new creature" (2 Cor. 5:17). As a Christian, the Holy Spirit dwells in me, "ye are not in the flesh, but in the spirit" (Rom. 8:9). I have a tremendous responsibility. Will Christ be magnified in my body?

After ten years in a traveling itinerate ministry, the Holy Spirit placed the desire inside me and opened the door to stay in one place. We were holding meetings at a church that didn't have a pastor. I was invited to stay on and continue the work. Our interim ministry period started. It came at a good time because my wife and I would soon be having our first child. In our first decade of ministry, we never were able to enter into personal issues and become involved with believers' problems. This would make it possible to build relationships and easier for a young family to live. In this village church, I discovered a lot of lost souls. They were unbelievers believing they were believers. The residence of the Holy Spirit was absent. This is rather shocking thing to share but it was the truth. They lost the idea that Jesus Christ is the head of the church and the church members are in a personal, committed, trusting relationship with Him. I was reminded "know ye not that your body is the temple of the Holy Ghost which is in you, which ye have of God and ye are not your own" (I Cor. 6:19).

The pastor's first priority is always to die to self, yield to God's will and be completely dedicated to his Lord and Savior. None of these important principles were in the village church. It really doesn't make any difference if the church is small or large. I have come to the conclusion that I must recognize the residence of the Holy Spirit. The church needed a reality check. I had to get down to the basics. It started with me. Do I realize that the God I love through Jesus Christ is dwelling in my very being, and am I living that out for all to see? I imagined what it would be like to deal with every part of life with His presence in me and the church.

We know so little about God. Even when I look into the solar system, I have really seen just the fringes of God. The God that lives in me is totally and absolutely complete within Himself. Nothing can be added to or taken away from God. I cannot box Him in. Everything that makes God who He is already resides within Him. I can believe or reject Him, but He is still God. God is not dependent on me. I am, we all are, dependent on Him. I have served in large and small churches. I hate to say it but when I failed, it was because I forgot that He resides in me. I have made mistakes but God forgives in our repentance and confession. The greater mistake is allowing Satan to use the mistake to focus on and keep me from God. The village church and I learned that we must daily recognize His divine presence.

The next part of the verse shows me how to live out the divine presence, "Be not conformed to this world but be ye transformed by the renewing of your mind." We must not only recognize the divine presence in us, but we must respond to the divine transformation. What does it mean to be Christ-centered? Is my lifestyle based upon the world's system of belief and values? Transformation is an ongoing experience. We manifest God's redemption through our redeemed nature. The world wants to control our minds but God wants to transform us from within. The Holy Spirit releases power from inside through our spirit. This takes place when I allow Jesus Christ to dominate my life through the saturation of His Word in my mind. Christianity is a process. I have learned that in everything Christ must be the focus.

In my first full-time pastorate, I learned what it means to allow the divine residence of the Holy Spirit to bring daily transformation. Jesus Christ has been the dominate means for daily alterations in my life. I had to learn to respond to the divine demands. God says "give me your body" and now He says "give me your mind." The Christian walk is hard and especially if you are a pastor. Every eye is upon you. When Jesus says to be meek, you'd better be gentle. If He says be humble, you'd better be careful when you are proud of something that the people don't take it out of context. When He says don't worry, you'd better be strong. If you sin, confess it but take into account who you are sharing it with.

At Eastport Baptist Church on Torch Lake, we settled into a period that covered almost a decade. It could have been many more years. It was a good place to go after short interim ministries. Just about everything I did at the church took a double meaning. The church became my graduate field project in ministry. "The Development of a Local Assembly" was my research-applied Christianity project. Being transformed myself and watching others grow in their discipleship became a careful spiritual and intellectual pursuit.

Transformation involves sound doctrine. I spent a whole year preparing and teaching Bible doctrine on Wednesday evenings. The development of a theological foundation was the starting point and the end product was a "Doctrinal Digest" manual and the Biblical resource to transform us. During this time, one of my church deacons came to me. He loved the Lord and was a servant of Jesus and His church. He was not aware of all the things he accomplished in helping me, his pastor and the church community. He asked if we could meet weekly for a time of spiritual conversation. He had many friends to talk to about community events, sports, hunting and so many other things. He was longing to talk about Jesus. Romans 12:2 was one of our dialogues and we both wanted to be transformed by the renewing of our minds. Paul says, "I urge you." He is urging us to listen, to respond and accept the gift of God. What is this gift? Our discussion led to the conclusion that we can receive a new 'electro-chemical computer' (brain-mind). Long ago people thought that the mind was an invisible inner representative of self and could be understood only by looking beyond humans for an explanation. The Greeks thought that the mind was a function of the body and that behavior was a product of the mind. Today we have many views of the mind and many different areas of study that relate to the mind. The mind and philosophy involve speculation. The mind and physiology involve observation. The mind and physics involve measurement. The mind and psychology involve testing. The mind and theology involve reconstruction. We were interested in the reconstruction part. We control our brain, our thinking and our emotion. We are directly responsible for our actions. We choose how we think and feel.

Difficulties are, for the most part, self-induced, self-maintained, self-magnified and self-distorted. My friend and I discussed how we could be free from anger, depression, envy, guilt, hatred, hostility and jealousy. It all depends on what we put our faith in. Faith requires an initiation, action and commitment.

All of this takes place in our minds. Everything we do ultimately is the result of our thoughts. What kind of mind do we want? The deacon and I wanted a renewed mind. This mind is a reflection of God's love (I John 3:23-24). I have to respond to God's demands and be under-girded by love. The renewed mind is a mind of obedience to God's commands in faith and love. It is the verification that God lives in this mind by the operating of God's spirit in our life. The renewing of our 'electro-chemical computer' (mind) is possible through faith, hope and trust. Transformation involves not only sound doctrine but the development of a Biblical organizational structure in the church. This took another year of teaching and concluded with a reliable church polity manual and behavioral strategy. Today there is increased confusion not only in regard to the great fundamentals of Christian faith but the organizational structure of the church. If the church is the assembly representing Jesus Christ, it must believe in the eternal deity of Jesus Christ, is virgin birth, His sinless life, His substitutionary and atoning death, His bodily resurrection, His high priestly ministry and His sure return. The church is going to believe in the verbal inspiration, inerrancy and complete authority of the Bible. It will have a regenerate membership based upon the individual and familial covenant with God through Jesus Christ and the Holy Spirit. The constitution and by-laws will transmit the supreme lordship of Jesus Christ and obedience to His will as revealed in the Bible. Jesus Christ is the master and there is no rule but His Word. I had an outstanding time in studying, discussing, evaluating and preparing a polity manual (behavioral digest).

The third section of the text says, "That ye may prove what is that good and acceptable and perfect will of God." I have thought about the divine residence, the divine transformation and now the divine will at work in me. God is working His will in me. He is making me like His dear Son. He is shaping me into the image of Christ. His presence, His transforming process and His will can be accomplished. I have learned that each day belongs to Him. His will is that I yield my agenda for the day to Him and let Him work it as He sees best. I have to keep in mind that He has my best interest in mind. I do not have to understand what is happening. He works in mysterious ways sometimes. His will is that I understand that the mind controls the body and the will controls the mind. His prayer is mine, "thy will be done."

A third year would involve an accountability strategy based on His will being accomplished. Many times I have worked really hard in trying to do God's will. I have tried to practice different formulas of my own to make it work. I have learned to just let go of self and let God do it. He is going to have His will accomplished. He is God. He does enable me to do His will. I have found victory, strength, courage and the knowledge to do His will.

We find this in Hebrews 13:20, 21. Let me pull each emphasis out of the text. "May the God of peace" is a phrase that says authority is found in our creator/ redeemer. He is the author and dispenser of peace. We can trust our lives to Him. Peace is the result of that trust. "Blood of the eternal covenant", the blood that Christ shed on the cross, secures God's promises for those who believe. I can rest on the decision of faith to rely on God's Word. His word is power. "Brought back from the dead", Jesus is the focus of this phrase. He is life because He conquered death. Enablement is mine through the power of the resurrection. If I believe in Christ and His power, I have access to the power of God. "Our Lord Jesus" is personal. I can enjoy my life in Christ because Jesus is Lord. He is superior and He is master. The "great shepherd", Christ, accomplished all His saving work and I have no needs that He cannot meet. He is the best caregiver. God will "equip you with everything good"; He prepares me and makes me fit and He will enable me for all I have to face. God prepares us "for doing His will and may He work in us what is pleasing to Him". Under the new covenant, He provides power to do His will and reveals His will. The key is to will my will to His. His will becomes my desire. "Through Jesus Christ" shows the emphasis not on receiving but on development. Development involves true sacrifice, obedience, discipline, fellowship and trust. "To whom be glory forever and ever", Jesus Christ is the object of glory. I have been invited to participate in God's plan to bring honor to Jesus. My entire life here and hereafter is to honor, glorify, praise and worship. When God says "Amen", it means "it is and shall be so." God will keep His promises and enable me to be all He wants me to be. His purpose will be established. I have chosen to agree with Him. "Thy will be done" means that now I watch His will at work in me.

My last full-time pastoral ministry took me into the most exciting time of my life. It would involve daily change, daily central focus and daily commitment. Mars Hill Bible Church started with several hundred people. In my former experience, churches began small and grew. I grew up thinking that a large church would be between 600 to 1,000 people. This church started at 600 in attendance. As Associate Pastor, my job every Sunday was to respond to the folks that requested assistance in their spiritual life. It was a church in fellowship. Small groups were started and eventually became house churches and a part of the larger assembly. It was a praying church. The small congregational groups became the prayer warriors for each member. It was a reverent church. It was not traditional but it was transparent. People came as they were to bow before Jesus Christ the head of the church. It was a church where things happen. This church believed that if we expect great things from God and attempt great things for God, things will happen. It was a sharing church. The believers had an intense feeling of responsibility for each other and it was a worshipping church. The people came from different backgrounds but had one thing in common. They came to worship. It was a happy church. We didn't have time to be gloomy with all the transformation taking place. It was a church that drew people. Real Christianity is a love affair.

On my first day of ministry, a young man came to me; in the previous week he had accepted Jesus Christ in his life. This week he brought a friend that needed the Savior. Right there in the hallway, his friend responded to the Holy Spirit's invitation. A continuous flow of needy souls followed this first example "thy will be done." We had hundreds of counseling sessions and with those sessions came opportunity to interview graduate students that were in an internship with us. We would see God's power in action in multiple ways. One of my greatest experiences was the participation in baptizing hundreds of people on a sunny, sandy shore. I will cherish the pictures and memories of the young and old who committed their lives to Jesus and demonstrated their obedience through baptism. It was like standing on the Jordan River in the wilderness and doing God's will. In my home study on the wall, there is a beautiful plaque that says "My heart leaps for joy and I give thanks to him in song" (Psalm 28:7). It has a musical lyre on it which emphasizes my musical proclamation of the Word and gives testimony of my first counselee at the church.

I was driving on 28th Street in Grand Rapids, Michigan and the teaching pastor of the church called me on my cell phone. He asked me if I had ever worked with someone that was having a battle with Satan, demon-possessed or under direct attack. It took me by surprise but it shouldn't have because we are always facing spiritual battles. I drove into a parking lot to give full attention to him. I thought for a moment and remembered that while I served at the Kalamazoo Gospel Mission, I had many opportunities to call on the name of Jesus for deliverance and protection. I told the pastor that I could help. He then told me that he had a man on the phone that needed God's help now! I told him to tell the guy to meet me at Meijer's parking lot. I began to pray and think about what was ahead of me.

The Bible says, "be of sober spirit, be on the alert, your adversary, the devil prowls about like a roaring lion seeking someone to devour" (I Peter 5:8). Satan's prime objective is the defeat of God. The Bible says, "we have authority over the enemy, behold I give unto you power to tread on serpents and scorpions and over all the power of the enemy, and nothing shall by any means hurt you." The word 'power' should be translated to 'authority'. It says, "behold I give you authority over the power of the enemy". The Christian does not have power over Satan. He has authority over Satan. The source of our authority over Satan is rooted in God and His power.

This first encounter caused many sessions on how to win, which is God's will for us. The gift was given for appreciation in sharing how to receive the victory. We must remain committed if we are going to win. Because of Christ's victory on the cross, we have a right to evict the thoughts that come from the flesh and the devil (2 Cor. 10:4-5). We must refocus our thought life, not to win the victory, but to receive the victory that has already been won. Only if we understand our authority can our minds be renewed. We must reprogram our minds with God's Word and His Word will increase our faith. The Bible says, "watch over your heart with all diligence, for from it flows the springs of life" (Proverbs 4:23). We must fill our minds with the wonder of Christ and desire to be like him. We must have verses of Scripture ready to quote at a moment's notice. We must always be ready to combat lies with the truth of God's Word. God himself must be first in our thinking. Are we fully committed to live to the praise of God's glory?

Do not run from Him when you fail but run to Him. After many sessions in discipleship, we discovered the divine residence, the divine transformation and the divine will. The proclamation of the Word will continue as the word of Christ dwells in me and as I respond to that word. "Worship the Lamb of Glory" with me.

TEN

DEAR LORD AND FATHER OF MANKIND
Matthew 6:12

The songwriter has written, "Dear Lord and Father of mankind, forgive our foolish ways, clothe us in our rightful mind...in deeper reverence, praise." My greatest delight is communicating to God. It is the highest and holiest privilege. If our spirit bears witness with His Spirit, we are His children (Matthew 6:9, 7:11). We can move to higher and deeper experiences in prayer. In the Garden of Gethsemane, "Jesus went a little farther and fell on His face and prayed" (Matthew 26:39). This is communion. It means deep fellowship (Revelation 3:20). It involves God the Father, the Son and the Holy Spirit (2 Corinthians 13:14). This prayer is my motivation to "pray continually." It is a state of the heart, a spontaneous beat. Praying is the breathing of the spirit. It should be natural and automatic in our daily experience. Let our hearts "pant after God" (Psalm 42:1). The communion stage takes us to "our Father...not my will but thy will be done." This prayer brings satisfaction, victory, joy and blessing.

The "forgive us our debts" brought me into this stage of prayer. The phrase refers to our sins of unrighteousness. He has given us the right to bring our daily acts of disobedience to Him. Confession of sin (to miss the mark) characterizes genuine Christianity. We are to confess our sins in order to obtain a day-to-day cleansing (I John 1:9). When Jesus gave his first sermon in his hometown of Nazareth, He said He came to release us from captivity of our sins (Luke 4:18, John 8:32).

The Bible says "Behold I was shapen in iniquity and in sin did my mother conceive me" (Psalm 51:5). This is in contrast to what we would like to hear. The word "sin" has been washed out of our vocabulary today. No group of people in the world is exempt from sin. It is at the heart of the troubles of the world. The first time that man had to make a choice between God's truth and the devil's lie, he chose the devil's lie. This is the moment that all the troubles of the world began. The sin problem is solved through Jesus Christ. If we do not believe in Him, we will die in our sins (John 8:24).

Habitual sin is incompatible with the ministry of the Holy Spirit. We are to exhibit righteous character (Galatians 5:22-23). Divine forgiveness paves the way to holy living. Through the acknowledgement of the Biblical truths concerning confession, forgiveness and justification, we are able to start the process. When our sin (debts) are released from us in forgiveness, we can live with honesty, confidence, self-esteem, acceptance and emotional stability.

As we forgive our debtors, there are two good ways to learn about forgiveness. We need to practice it and experience it. Do not become rigid, condemning, demanding and unforgiving but show love, give encouragement and accept weaknesses. Deep relationships with other people are one of God's ways of making us strong and whole (2 Peter 1:8). The Bible does not say we should run around telling our problems to everyone we meet, but it does say we should "bear each other's burdens."

I have never doubted God's forgiveness. I believe in what He says which pardons us from sin and disobedience through confession. I have worked with many people that have found it hard to believe that God would cancel their sins through Christ's blood. Constantly, their sins hound them. Their physical and mental scars are a reminder. Prevention is a good thing to apply to one's life. Consequences of wrong decisions can bring much pain.

My problem has never been with the promise of release but to renounce the sin or wrongdoing. To cut it off and to disown it has continued to be a problem. A double attack has taken place and my own sensitivity to wanting righteousness and the stain of wrongdoing is a reminder. The guilt has led to self-blame, self-condemnation, feelings of worthlessness and borderline depression. I live with the goal of having an upright character. It is the most important quality to have. A Biblical solid character has always been my goal. If it is tarnished no matter what, it causes grief and pain. Satan knows exactly how to hinder my spiritual lifestyle. Learning to reject the thoughts that caused me to doubt became a training field. Learning to renounce reminders that short-change my life becomes an ongoing battleground; keeping me from realizing that the blood of Christ has erased any wrongdoing. My super-sensitive nature gets wounded. After much time of struggle and contemplation on how to refuel, I obtain the victory. I am able through the Holy Spirit's enablement to release, renounce and refuel, gaining a spiritual vitality. If you have had a battle in this line of thought, do not be discouraged. God is immensely able to give you the victory. Like me, you have to decide to accept what God has to say and act on it. The Holy Spirit will step in and carry you along the way through grace.

ELEVEN

SPIRIT OF GOD DESCEND UPON MY HEART
Luke 24:49

The songwriter has written, "Spirit of God descend upon my heart…and make me love Thee as I ought to love." Jesus said, "I have come that ye may have life and have it to the full" (John 10:10). The Gospel of John is a favorite among Christians. Its purpose is found in three key words: signs, belief and life. Eight signs and miracles prove Jesus' deity. We can trust in who He is and what He has done. 'Believe' refers to trust, commit, and receive. These words emphasize our responsibility. Jesus Christ is the son of God. We must believe in Him. 'Life' is the result of belief. We become a new creation (II Cor. 5:17) when we believe. Eternal life has begun in us through faith. The full life refers to abundance and completeness. It is a life that is satisfied and contented. When we came into a vital union with the risen Lord we became a new creation (John 3:3; 15:5; Galatians 6:14-15).

We are able to live this life daily when we accept the promise of the Father (Luke 24:49) and act on His promises. Jesus said "...I send the promise of my Father upon you: but tarry ye in the city of Jerusalem until ye be endued with power from on high". The promise involves the indwelling presence of the Holy Spirit mentioned the night before Christ's crucifixion (John 16:7-15). "I go away...I will send the comforter to you". "The spirit of truth will guide you into all truth" (John 16:13). He says, "I will instruct you and teach you in the way you should go. I will counsel you and watch over you" (Psalm 32:8).

Keep in mind to understand the supreme being, spiritual transformation is necessary (John 3:7). Spiritual knowledge comes through spiritual illumination. If we experience despair, be comforted because the encourager has come. If we lack confidence, remember we have an advocate. If we live with worry, keep in mind that ultimate truth lies in the self-revelation of God. The divine genius provides guidance not delusion. He equips us with discernment not falsehood. He will give wisdom not folly. We may live in perilous times with distortion and deception, but God the Father has promised the Holy Spirit and Jesus Christ the Son has sent Him to us. He is only a breath away. Let's refuse confusion and the terror of the unknown and allow the presence of the Almighty, the Holy Spirit, to supply our needs.

The Holy Spirit is our encourager, comforter, advocate, intercessor and helper. There is no one like Him. He is not a divine influence or power. He is a divine person of infinite majesty and glory and holiness and power. A person is defined as one who has knowledge, feeling and a will. This is what is stated of the Spirit (John 14:16-18): He comforts, bears witness, is equal to the Father and Son, appears in different visible forms, can be offended, and offers special individual gifts according to His own will. The divine helper is God. He has the same qualities. He has the same work. When we recognize the Holy Spirit as a person and recognize His deity, we can respond to His activities. Jesus said with his own lips that the Holy Spirit is divine. He said to his disciples that he would send "another counselor" (John 14:16).

The word 'another' means another just like the first one. Jesus said that he would send a person just like Himself, one that is fully divine. The work of the Holy Spirit is given by Jesus Christ (John 16:13-14). The primary work is to glorify Christ. All His works are included within this one. He bears witness of Jesus (John 15:26) through teaching, drawing people to Christ, reproducing the character of Christ, giving guidance for service and providing sustaining power.

To live the Christ-glorifying life, we must be filled with the Holy Spirit. The Holy Spirit is Christ's representative in our hearts. He points the way. He answers for Christ in every situation we face. When we yield to the leadership of the comforter, we honor our Lord. The Holy Spirit in our life is Christ Himself among us. The road to victory and triumph and glory in life is through the indwelling Holy Spirit. The Bible says, "Know ye not that your body is the temple of the Holy Ghost that is in you?" (I Cor. 6:19). He doesn't dwell in the soul, mind or conscience but in the body. We had better pay attention to our physical senses: what we see, touch, feel or what we read, look at, hear and where we go with our feet. We belong to Jesus Christ. We have been bought with a price. The Holy

Spirit indwells us to represent our owner; our body has become His temple. As we live in the present, be reminded that our souls have been quickened from a state of spiritual death (Eph. 2:5) and our bodies shall live in the resurrection life in the likeness of Christ (Phil. 3:21). This provides much joy and encouragement as we face hardships. As Christians we have a body that has become the Holy Spirit's residence. The inner man is strengthened with might by His Spirit (Eph. 3:16). This strength will reproduce the character of Christ in us. The fruit of the spirit is the result of His indwelling. As we look up to Him, we arc empowered. It's not working on becoming like Jesus Christ. It's setting our affections, our minds on things above where Christ is.

To experience the full, abundant, complete life, we have to learn to make some important decisions on a daily basis. A friend of mine said, "Faith is a decision to respond correctly to God." Conversion is a decision to receive (John 3:16), consecration is a decision to surrender (Romans 12:1-2), cleansing is a decision to confess (I John 1:9), and claiming is a decision to accept (John 12:48). "Faith is the response of the total person to God as a person in loving submission, trust, and obedience. This is in and through the person of Jesus as the revelation of God and redeemer of mankind, who is the sovereign Lord, who offers Himself to the believer, through the ministry of the Holy Spirit and the Scriptures, as his daily sufficiency."

Every believer should obey, there is no exception. It is a distinct duty. It means to keep on being filled moment by moment. We have to be willing to be saturated with the Holy Spirit. When we become willing, He will fill us with His presence and power. The key question is: does He have all of us?

Our goal is to respond to God's Word in the correct way through "being filled with the Holy Spirit". 'Being filled' requires belief, submission, confession and claiming; these are essential for soul-care ministers. The "Promise of the Father" (Luke 24:49) is the indwelling presence of the Holy Spirit. He will watch over us (Psalm 32:8). He definitely has been my encourager, comforter, advocate, intercessor and helper. He has helped me to glorify Jesus Christ. Faith is defined in making decisions. "To be filled by the spirit" (Ephesians 5:18) requires four decisions: 1) conversion, a decision to receive, 2) consecration, a decision to surrender, 3) cleansing, a decision to confess, and 4) claiming, a decision to accept.

Many years ago I had completed ten years in a traveling ministry. Preaching and music were integrated into a church-wide ministry. Our first child was going to be born and the Lord provided a way to help us settle into a small church in southern Michigan. As the village parson, I was called upon for everything that needed a minister. I was called to the hospital to visit unknown individuals, I was called to serve the family that lost their son to death through an accident who was considered as the town drunk. I had to assist in my first drug addiction case and was called to visit and officiate at a teen suicide funeral.

The list is long but the most vivid occasion that came to my mind regarding the Holy Spirit and His indwelling power was at a graduation ceremony. Since this first experience, I have had many opportunities as the town pastor. I was invited to give the invocation at a multimillion dollar high school building site. As I approached the platform and looked out at the huge attendance, I requested through prayer to my heavenly Father that it would be great to preach at their first baccalaureate graduation ceremony. I thought just think of the glory that Jesus Christ would receive and I was so excited about this request that I started preparing a sermon for the occasion. A few weeks after the building dedication, I received a call to speak at the graduation ceremony. The Lord answered my prayer. I began to get nervous about speaking to such a large audience and became concerned about my responsibility to the Lord. I like to study and prepare sermons. This is easy for me. After many hours of preparing, I knew what I should share with those teenagers and parents who would be present at the ceremony. I became more and more uneasy. The day of the graduation, I preached a sermon for my own church and after the service I became ill. I rested and let my whole being flow into the Spirit's hands. I spoke out loud and said that all I wanted to do was to glorify my Lord Jesus Christ and to reach the community for Him. I needed peace and rest and boldness. I had to lead those graduates into the huge auditorium with confidence with a positive authority of the power of the Holy Spirit. I then said, "I claim your indwelling presence – do as you wish with this humble preacher. Please let souls be saved and Christians be challenged."

As I began to let go of myself and submit to a total dependence, I started to sense a release of worry, sickness and an overwhelming lack of control. It must be similar to a paralyzed condition: no feeling, no control, no independence. I was overcome with a sense of peace, rest and spiritual boldness. I entered the auditorium and led the youth and administration to the platform. When it was time for me to speak, I looked at my watch. I spoke for forty minutes and do not remember what I said. I had prepared well, everything was memorized and held my Bible open and referred to it several times. I spoke with ease and when I finished, the response followed through the next few weeks. Community members were excited about what they heard and the graduates consulted me to make decisions to follow Jesus. The administration and staff were interested in discussing the topic I spoke on which was John 14:6. I was so delighted that the Holy Spirit entered into this special opportunity. In simple humility, I claimed His presence and power and something happened. It will happen to you as well when you seek the helper. He is only a breath away.

TWELVE

HEAR OUR PRAYER, O LORD
Psalm 34:15; Matthew 6:11

The songwriter has written, "Hear our prayer, O God, incline thine ear to us and grant us thy peace." The first half of the Lord's Prayer focuses on God. The believer has the privilege to come to God. I have discovered that prayer is found in three stages: petition, communion and intercession. It is a developmental process as well as a united focus. The petition stage involves coming to God with my personal needs and making my requests known to Him on the basis of His promises. The communion stage involves fellowship. It is an intimate spiritual intercourse with God. Intercession reaches out to others.

A petition is a request. It means asking or craving. It is a plea. Praying is supplicating God for His help and grace. It is a plea of the soul to deity. It involves both spiritual and temporal. As a spiritual infant, I began by coming to God with my needs. "Our Father, give us this day our daily bread." The physical needs are brought to His attention. The simple word to designate this stage is "ask." Jesus said, "Ask, and it shall be given you; seek, and ye shall find; knock, and it shall be opened unto you. For everyone that asks receives; and he that seeks finds, and to him that knocks, it shall be opened" (Matthew 7:7,8). He said, "ask and ye shall receive." God's promise is clear and simple. "The eyes of the Lord are upon the righteous and His ears are open unto their cry" (Psalm 34:15).

"Give us this day our daily bread" refers to all of man's physical needs. We are dependent on Him. In a previous pastoral ministry, I was asked by a medical doctor to visit one of his patients at the hospital. It was a young man that had been in a terrible accident and was paralyzed from the neck down. He had been an athlete and had a body and physical attributes that anyone would envy. In the week of his accident, he was going to get married. The accident put a stop to all his dreams. He wished that he could erase this period of his life. His fiancé was in good health, but, of course, was discouraged and depressed.

I did not want to visit that scene and I prayed to get out of this request. I did not know what to say in such a hopeless situation. My heart got in the way of my reasoning and excuse-making. As I walked into the hospital, I came up with a few more reasons not to visit, but then I decided to give in to God's will. I prayed with deep sincerity that God would intervene. I even lost my way in the hospital and then found myself praying that I would find the man. I finally found the room and God took over as I walked in his room. A sense of peace came over me and my thoughts were centered around "thy will be done" and "give us this day our daily physical needs." Boldness in the Holy Spirit and confidence overpowered my weaknesses.

As I walked into the patient's room, it was crowded with hospital staff and with tact and confidence, they seemed to think I was a medical specialist. I was a specialist but in the spiritual realm. I approached the young man with his fiancé standing at the side of his bed and introduced myself. I made reference to the medical doctor who invited me to visit. The personnel in the room moved out of the way and gave me space. The room became very quiet and a special light seemed to appear. The room had a special guest as God was making His presence known. As I introduced myself, I automatically held the hand of the young man even though he couldn't feel it, but he could see it. I completely forgot myself and my inadequacies and looked straight into his eyes. I knew God could help bring peace and even a miracle if he desired. I thought about "our Father who art in heaven" and "the Lord is my shepherd, I shall not want." In one thought we have the power source and in the other, we have the promise. The young man at that moment had an awareness of God's enablement. I wiped away his tears and prayed for deliverance, patience, courage and, most of all, for God's will to be done. The young man whispered in my ear, "I think a miracle has taken place." He discovered peace and the will to go through with this new life-consuming challenge and leave it in God's hands and not his own. I thanked the medical personnel and left with an unspeakable blessing.

THIRTEEN

WHAT A FRIEND WE HAVE IN JESUS
Psalm 71:5; Romans 5:13

The songwriter has written, "What a friend we have in Jesus, all our sins and griefs to bear. What a privilege to carry, everything to God in prayer." In my youth I read this promise, "For thou art my hope, O Lord God; thou art my trust from my youth" (Psalm 71:5). Recently I read "The God of hope fill you with all joy and peace in believing that you may abound in hope through the power of the Holy Ghost" (Romans 15:13). I have appreciated this promise and hope to continue to seek it, claim it, and hold onto it for daily encouragement. There are no uncertainties in God's path. I am secure because Jesus Christ is my security and friend.

Hope is a confident expectation and anticipation that God will do what He says He will do. It is not wishful thinking. I am glad this text became rooted in my life as a youth. I am even glad that I can return to my childhood belief system. It is simple and easy to understand. I would like to share what I have learned as a child and teenager in regard to hope. I would also like to illustrate that instruction with adult experiences.

My hope is built upon the presence of the Holy Spirit. Our finite minds cannot grasp the infinity of God. We cannot fully comprehend this truth because of our limitations. But as a child and young adult, I can believe and live in the light of it. The Scripture says, "Do you not know that your body is a temple of the Holy Spirit, who is in you, whom you have received from God? You are not your own and you were bought at a price. Therefore, honor God with your body" (I Corinthians 6:18-20). I know that this is true because I have the witness of the Holy Spirit in me (Romans 8:15-17). The Holy Spirit has joined my spirit in testifying that I am His child. This inner witness of the spirit accounts for the peace and confidence that I have. I have learned to take God at

His Word. Through accepting the Lord Jesus as my Savior, the Holy Spirit has brought His supernatural peace and unwavering confidence to my heart and mind. Studying God's Word, applying it to my life and continuing conversations with God have brought confirmation. Spiritual certainty is accomplished through constant fellowship with Jesus Christ. Only the Holy Spirit can give assurance and certainty. My effort is not sufficient. The inner witness will come as I desire to obey the Lord in complete trust.

In this day of discontent, discouragement, disconnectedness, depression and just plain hopelessness, hope can still become a reality. If the world rubs off on me with inadequacies, I have the Holy Spirit that intercedes for me (Romans 8:26, 27). If physical pain or emotional distress come upon me, the Spirit prays for me. The indwelling Holy Spirit understands me and knows what is best for me. After filtering out all selfish and sinful elements, He presents my inner longings to the Father.

With the indwelling of the Holy Spirit, I can "abound in hope" through His power. I carry in my billfold a little card that says, "Pastoral Prescription", a power source. I started this ministry many years ago. On pastoral visitation calls, I would always leave a card for encouragement to people. I would ask for discernment and sensitivity for the need and then I would leave the prescription card with the promise that it would edify the people that I visited. The card in my pocket has only three Biblical references on it but with the understanding that the Holy Spirit indwells me. I pray the references into reality. They are Ephesians 5:18 "be filled with the Spirit," I John 1:9 "confess sin, He will forgive," and Luke 11:9-10, 13 "ask and receive." Whatever I face, I can apply the Biblical perspective. The promise of hope is activated.

Being in-between pastoral ministries can be a time of refreshment and a refuel process or it can be distasteful, doubtful and uneasy. It depends upon the reason for leaving the previous ministry. It depends upon the attitude of the mind and upon the family, friendship and team workers encouragement. I seemed to have some opportunities but they did not fit. The Lord led me to a third shift security job and I did not like it, but food was necessary for the table. It did provide time for reflection, study and meditation. I love animals and was given, when on duty, a German shepherd dog to be my helper. We got along very well and I felt secure because he could tell if anyone was out in the dark or around unseen corners. Wherever I went on patrol in the car or on foot, he was at my side. He was a good companion in good and bad situations. Today I would take my own dog. Hunter is a chocolate lab and has already shown skills in giving support.

But the dog assigned to me became sick and I had to patrol alone. It was a dark and dense foggy evening and I received a call to investigate the property because there was a person or group sneaking around the area. I had to enter territory that could be dangerous. I needed help to step out and the verse came to my mind in Exodus 23:22, "if thou shall indeed obey His voice and do all that I speak, then I will be an enemy unto thine enemies and an adversary unto thine adversaries." At the time, it seemed reassuring that God could be an enemy to my enemy. "The Lord your God goeth before you" (Deuteronomy 1:30). "The Almighty shall be thy defense" (John 22:25). My hope and confidence was in God's Word. I would obey His voice and ask to be filled with the Spirit. I would confess any wrongdoings and be clean before Him, and then I would ask for Him to protect me and give me safety and courage to step out and face whatever was waiting for me. His power gave me a sense of peace and, in belief, I went out into the dangerous dark unknown path. I reminded the Lord that I was His temple and if I would get hurt, it was alright because He knows best if I understand or not. It definitely was scary but I felt that I could have encountered anything and I would have been victorious. The police came and made an arrest and I left with joy because I learned to have hope in God's Word and was confident in my friend Jesus.

FOURTEEN

LEANING ON THE EVERLASTING ARMS
2 Timothy 1:17

The songwriter has written "What have I to dread, what have I to fear, leaning on the everlasting arms. I have blessed peace with my Lord so near, leaning on the everlasting arms." It has always been hard for me to open up and share, even though I have shared many times in witnessing. Every ministry position I have held has brought new delicate, difficult, and sometimes dangerous challenges. Confrontation and debate with an agreeable taste is alright but when does that ever happen? Because of my super-sensitive nature, I can disagree agreeably. I really have to rely upon 2 Timothy 1:7 which says "God hath not given me the spirit of fear."

I am able to establish a daily bold witness through applying the text. To overcome personal weaknesses and inadequacies, I must be conscious of God's presence. If I am fearful, lack confidence or just feeling uneasy, I must place myself into the text and share with the Holy Spirit who is my comforter. I have to claim the verse for every activity. I have to pray for the right opportunities to come to my attention. I must ask for God's courage and boldness. I must respond with love for Jesus Christ and be ready to glorify Him. I must be sound in my judgment and be prepared with the strength of the Holy Spirit. When I lean on "the everlasting arm" of the Lord, the promise will be fulfilled.

I have seen it work in a variety of experiences. In music, I have created, developed and established many instrumental music education curriculums. I have prayed for the right opportunity and through certain circumstances, they have opened up. When I started the programs at some of the schools, I was driving past the school and an inner voice, my subconscious, told me to stop and investigate the opportunity. I asked for courage and God's power and when I asked to talk with the administrator, he was already prepared for me. The administration and other officials had previously discussed the idea but did not know what step to take after that. I was able to establish the curriculum because God gave me a passion and love for music and children. I realized that students should have the right to glorify God in this way. I think the Lord gave me boldness to enter unknown territory because of the love He had produced in me. He also gave a sound mind and good judgment to me. The development of self-confidence through knowledge and previous preparations prepared the way. I did not have to enter into the opportunity with embarrassment because I was confident in what I was doing. God had promised the spirit of fearlessness. Power, strength, courage, boldness, love, passion, deep desire and a sound mind have been integrated together to bring success. "O how sweet [it is] to walk in this pilgrim way." It is fellowship with Jesus that makes it possible.

In ministry, this verse has paid big dividends. I was on the way to visit a family from my church because pastoral visitation was a worthwhile ministry in my church. I have always been organized and was following my agenda. This family was on the list to visit. As I traveled, I reached the top of the hill and came to a four-way stop. I had been praying for the right thing to talk about and would always leave a pastoral prescription with encouragement. My thoughts were deep in listening to the Lord. My spirit kept saying that I should turn left instead of right to the family's home. If I turned to the left, I would end up at the hospital. I didn't have anyone at the hospital to visit at this time. This would mess up my schedule, but the urge was so great that I was compelled to turn toward the hospital. I took an aggressive step and followed the inner voice.

When I reached the hospital, a nurse was waiting to direct me to a hospital room where a patient had asked for me. She was dying and was encouraged, by listening to a combined church music cantata that I had directed, to call for my presence. My visit was welcomed and spirit-led. After our visit, the Lord gave her peace and rest on her last few hours on earth. She would be soon in the very presence of her Savior. I was conscious of the Lord's presence. I was willing to follow whatever God wanted even if it didn't follow my previously prepared plan. I was in tune with His will. I walked into unknown territory without fear because the Holy Spirit was present with His power. I lost myself to the need of the hour and how I could be a servant to this dear lady that needed security and a sense of God's presence. I do not remember what was said but sound judgment and spiritual enlightenment was shared. The love of God was manifested and it motivated my direction into this changed plan of action. The Lord does not give fear but confidence as we fulfill His plan and rely on Him.

FIFTEEN

O HOW I LOVE JESUS
1 John 4:19

The songwriter has written "Love Divine, so great and wondrous, deep and mighty, pure, sublime, coming from the heart of Jesus, just the same thru' test of time." I remember singing this song from my heart. I love the words "like a dove when hunted, frightened, as a wounded fawn was I, brokenhearted, yet He healed me." I know what that feels like and I have walked through that same feeling with many others. This is the reason why I can sing, "O how I love Jesus…there is a name I love to hear, I love to sing its worth. It sounds like music in mine ear, the sweetest name on earth." Everybody has a different view of love. I can't think of anyone in my acquaintance that wouldn't want some loving.

Our society certainly has a confused view of it. What is love? The final authority has to be God. The Bible says, "We love because He first loved us" (I John 4:19). He also said, "I will show you the most excellent way" (I Cor. 12:31-13). Personally, I want to know "the most excellent way." My love story starts here. I have been on a journey with Jesus Christ. Whenever I need an answer on some important issue, I have made it a habit to discuss it with Him. The Scripture is His word given to me. In I John 4, it clearly states that God is the source of love. The origin of love comes from our creator, the infinite being who is self-existent, self-sustaining and eternal. Human love is a reflection of something in the divine nature itself. In Genesis 1:26, it says that we are in the image of God and in I John 4:16, it says "He who dwells in love dwells in God." We can see that there is a double relationship. Love comes from God and love leads to God. In my relationship with Jesus Christ, I have the capacity to love. God is known through love (v.12). You cannot see the wind but you can see the result of it. You cannot see the Spirit but you can sense His presence. You cannot see electricity but you can experience the effects of it. God shows His love through the demonstration of His Son. God held nothing back in giving His Son as a sacrifice for us. Human love is a response to that divine love (v.19).

My love journey in the marriage relationship had a foundation when I realized that God made me with a spirit, soul and body. The three parts of me were activated with the three components of love. Love is defined with self-giving and sacrifice (spiritual). Love is defined with friendship and companionship (soul). Love is defined with romantic attraction (physical). In marriage, when love has its roots and foundation in Jesus Christ, He will unite two individuals into a oneness without losing the identity of each soul. Someone said, "every person needs to receive love and to give love." I felt ready but questioned, "When will my turn come?"

My gospel team had just completed an engagement at a church and we decided to hang out at a restaurant for some refreshments. Many young people made it a habit to get together at this place. It was a good place to relax and I was sitting at my table looking at the menu when I looked up and, in a moment of amazement, saw her! I said in my heart, she is the one for me. She was leaving with some friends and she had on a blue and white sailor outfit. She had a smile on her face. Her hair was blond and I could even see her blue-green eyes. I thought for a moment, "I know her". We grew up in the same neighborhood and I would walk my dog past her house. Sometimes I would, without her knowing, listen to her practice the piano. She was a good pianist. Time had slipped by and she had grown up into a very pretty young woman. Everything I saw was delightful. I hadn't seen her or perhaps noticed her for several years. I thought that I needed to ask her out on a date. Sometimes when you really want to be with someone, it is hard to take that first step. I gathered up the nerve and called her. I asked her out to dinner and she turned me down. What a let-down! But I didn't give up and now I am glad that I didn't. She had a good excuse. She said she had to work but the real reason was because of the dental work she recently had done. I was definitely attracted to her. This could become a romantic journey. I finally got a date and we hit it off right from the start. "The Sound of Music" was the first movie we saw together and I got to hold her hand. We reflect on our getting together every time we think of that movie.

During that first summer, we spent a lot of time at the beach. I will have to be honest that she looked good in that swimming suit. After several dates, it seemed that our relationship was growing into friendship. A lasting companionship would develop. We both knew what true marriage was about. Oneness was the key. Our continued relationship was moving toward that objective.

The third love word given in the Scripture has to do with self-giving. This commitment is produced through Christ. His love is unconditional. Our love would be unconditional and possible because He infuses us with it. The Scripture says, "We love, because He first loved us" (I John 4:19). After dating the summer of 1966, we knew that God's love was being produced in our relationship. All the three loves were blended together into one activity. Love was being demonstrated in us through dating, engagement and marriage.

Up to this time, I was busy with my 'triple torch' career. The gospel team, school and business kept me on the move. Dating was fun and I liked being with the opposite sex, but I had many goals to reach. The Lord knew what He was doing in that this girl would have the personality, gifts, abilities and attitude to help me reach God's plan for both of us (Jeremiah 29:11). I was on the same journey that I started when I was sixteen. With her presence, joy was fulfilled. The love of my life in marriage was given the name 'Joy by her godly parents. We can spell love with happiness. I began a journey that would travel down nearly five decades so far.

I am sad when I am separated from her and will seek every opportunity to be with her. I remember when we first started to date that I would make secret visits to the hospital where she worked just to get a glimpse of her. This desire has never changed. Even now, I am lost without her and will call when it's really not necessary but I need to hear her voice. I may stop what I'm doing and just go to where she is. I really didn't think about love, marriage or family before I met Joy. Apparently, God's timing is perfect. When I saw her, I began to think about those things.

I asked the Lord to give me the desire and open up the opportunities. Happiness certainly would ring out clearly for both of us. I presented myself acceptably to her parents as they invited me over for a steak dinner (my favorite) soon after we showed interest in each other. We grew up at the same church and our parents were both active in the church. Her parents were active with youth and missions and mine were active in children's church and music. I knew in the first few dates that we had many things in common. The most important was our relationship with God. This would always take priority for both of us. I had often thought that if I ever had children, I would want them with Joy. Her purity in thought and body is a virtue that characterizes her life. Her standards have demonstrated her love for Jesus and have displayed genuine Christianity.

The word 'pride' demonstrates love. I have always been proud of her. I met her and started dating when she worked as a nurse at the hospital. She spent 20 years in the health services as a nurse and medical secretary. She has kept her nursing license up. Annual fees have been paid and new trends have come to her doorstep. She has been efficient and disciplined at her jobs. She has always moved forward in responsibility and advancement. She has not only been active in a career but active in the church, in raising the family, in being a wife and in assisting me with my studies and work. Her sacrifice has allowed our children to go to college and graduate without big cost factors.

After returning to Grand Rapids to care for her parents, she applied her clerical skills to the church. I visited Calvary Church and, after talking to several of the staff, discovered that there was an opening. With administrative, secretarial skills and having been a pastor's wife, she would be a great candidate for the position. She should fit in quite well. After much prayer, she interviewed and accepted the position. This would add another 20 years to her second career. I am proud of her achievements and ministry in a mega-church that she has been at for so many years. She has been able to accomplish this tenure because of her training, confidence, steadfastness, efficiency, with over-arching joy in her duties as she let God take charge. Jesus Christ is the head of the church and her boss.

Honesty plays an important part in dating. It's a virtue that should continue through life. We both grew up understanding that there is no such thing as a gray lie or black. When you lie, you lie. It is falsehood. You can't build anything with lies except more lies. It will catch up to you. God has always blessed truth even when it might hurt. Many times we have had to stand for truth. Honesty will ultimately win. I think we were drawn closer together because of these experiences. It did take some time to forgive. In understanding the issues and personalities behind the falsehood, we were able to confront the issues and move on. Releasing is forgiving. There were valuable lessons to learn. As a matter of fact, in ministry I had to counsel a chronic liar. The person lived a lie. I had to try to discover when this person was lying. Unfortunately, we live in a day that honesty is good only when it gives us something.

In dating, engagement, marriage or any relationship, we need to practice being honest. Living with a clear conscience brings wholesomeness. It helps you feel well physically. It gives you peace of mind. It brings a union together. These are steps toward oneness in marriage. In dating, we found happiness and joy. We found pride in knowing each other and in our separate accomplishments. We have practiced honesty in everything. This truly has become an exciting trip.

Our dating experience was great but our engagement period was greater. The one would build upon the other. Many words describe love in this time but the three that follow are at the top of the list: affection, adjustments and acceptance. I have had many people use the word love in a lot of different ways. Too often, it has been used without its true meaning and with haste. The word 'love' means a lot to me. I am not going to use it without some depth. It didn't take me long to know that love was developing in Joy's and my relationship, but it took some time for me to say, "I love you". Once I said it, I haven't stopped (my goal has been to tell her every day). I am a very affectionate person by nature. I have shown this affection through being polite, thoughtful and appreciative. I have been tender, close and physical and yet always with respect and adoration. Every action came from the heart. When it came time to propose, we were both ready for the question and answer. I told her that I loved her and she would be precious to me always. I chose my words carefully and deliberately. She accepted my love.

Our affection for each other was based upon our love relationship with God. God brought us together and He sustains us during life. Throughout all these years, we have to admit that He is the reason for our success. He has been working through us to accomplish His will and good pleasure. The fact is we love God with our whole heart, soul and mind. We know everything in our Christian life, everything about knowing Him and experiencing Him, and everything about knowing His will depends on the quality of our love relationship to Him. We discovered that our love relationship with God is more important than any other single factor in life. When that relationship is real and close, He will infuse us with love for each other. Out of His love for us, He provides all our needs to those who love Him and Him alone (Matt 6:31-33). It was during our dating and engagement period this foundation was built. He said "do not worry" and we still ask what shall we eat? Or what shall we drink? Or what shall we wear? Your heavenly Father knows your needs. "Seek first His kingdom and His righteousness and all these things will be given to you" (Matt 6:31-33). God did not create us for time; He created us for eternity. Time, our lifetime on earth, provides the opportunity to get acquainted with Him. It is an opportunity for

Him to develop our character in His likeness. Then eternity will have its fullest dimensions for us. If we just live for time (the here and now) we will miss the ultimate purpose of creation. If we live for time, we will allow our past to mold and shape our life today. Our lives, as children of God, ought to be shaped by the future (what we will be one day). God uses our present time to mold and shape our usefulness here on earth and in eternity. As we love one another in His love, we are learning to invest our life, time and resources on things that are lasting and not on things that will pass away. We have learned that He knows what is best for us. He has guided and He will continue to guide our togetherness and our affection for one another.

As Joy and I grew into the engagement period, we became more open to one another. In dating, there were blind spots. We just didn't see everything but now things began to open up. We were able to discuss personality and differences in men and women. Change and adjustment had to take place. Every time God spoke to people in the Scripture about something He wanted to do through them, major adjustments were necessary. In belief, we must

146

believe God is who He says He is and that He will do what He says He will do. Without faith in God, we will make wrong decisions. Actions will demonstrate our faith. In understanding, we will make the correct adjustments. We will have our preferences on issues and they can be handled with compromise. We have convictions that are similar. We have absolutes that we have in common. It was good to learn to adjust and make changes early because they became stepping stones for later.

I am going to share only about adjustments by giving them in different categories. I remember needing to learn that marriage is oneness. We cleave to one another and not to parents, friends or any other trusted soul. My mate is my closest companion. We had to deal with manipulation problems. It seemed that I had to play a balancing act on life to keep peace. This became better when control was released with love and a heart of concern. My personality, duty or interest didn't change because I got married. My wife became a helpmate - not an enemy, distraction or hindrance to my other relationships.

Traditions are great activities but they have to be given in love, not necessity. We join one another not because of duty but because of genuine interest in all parties. Most of our holidays became experiences of time scheduling. Every minute would be considered. Each family must have their due time. Living out of town created more problems. Having young children would constitute other issues. The balancing act was instituted. It seemed that we always made it. It was always good to see everyone. I think more transparency, openness and understanding are important elements which bring success.

We made some changes to circumstances of finances. I have been in business and have had to take care of a lot of money. At the end of the day, the account had to balance out. I didn't do too bad at this but didn't like the book work. I would rather work with people. The job of making sure every cent was accounted for was not my bag of interest. In our engagement period, we discussed the money matters. Of course, we didn't make very much money so this should have been an easy task. We know budgeting is essential to have family operations run smoothly. My dear wife was offered the job to keep things in order. Through the years, she has proven that she is at the top of the class in caring for money matters. I have taken the responsibility as president. Everything bad or good will drop in my lap. The stress, anxiety or worry needs to be mine and not hers. She is only carrying out certain duties that she is quite qualified to do. She has never made any big mistakes in the money issue. If anything, she has made the money go further. I appreciate this adjustment that turned out successfully.

We had to make some adjustment in our lifestyle in regard to our commitment to job, church and personal plans. We have always built on the philosophy that God is first in our devotion, that family is second in our dedication and the job is third in duty. All of our decisions were made with that focus in mind. A big change was made when Joy was working at the hospital. Many weekends involved work. My weekends were in ministry at the church. After prayer and discernment, we both decided that the hospital work should be replaced with medical office responsibilities. This turned out well because then Joy could be a part of the ministry that she couldn't in our dating period. She has contributed much to the Lord's work with me in addition to having her own ministry position at a church.

The affection that we have for each other has helped us make the adjustments that are necessary in our lives. These adjustments based on our preferences, convictions and absolutes have produced acceptance. We have learned to accept the imperfections, habits and differences. There are some things to cry about and other things to laugh about.

Our personalities are different but they complement each other. Her solid rock foundation puts roots to my creative and sometimes unreachable dreams. When you add Biblical transformation to the growth process, it brings an exciting journey into reality. We are at retirement age that doesn't mean that retirement is for us. We were living in a condominium. This part of our journey was very busy. I was at a mega-church and a consultant at a business. Joy was ministering at another mega-church. We were doing good things. I was trying to live by a 'be and do' philosophy of life. I promoted this kind of lifestyle. We must be what God wants us to be before we can do what He wants us to do. Constant fellowship and abiding in Jesus will bring unlimited possibilities. Being and doing must be balanced or failure will arrive on the doorstep.

The Lord provided the need (loss of money) to slow us up and to generate new beginnings. We sold our condominium and bought a piece of property to build a house. The house would become our place of ministry to integrate our tutoring and mentoring outreach. It took growth in faith to step out again to do this. Losing money that seemed to be security didn't help either. Both the rock-solid foundation and creative desire would be in God's planning. These would come together to glorify Jesus Christ and bring blessing to us, being safe in His arms. The acceptance of both strengths would unite and bring solidarity in our relationship. There are many things to accept in a relationship. When you start with the right foundation which is biblically orientated, life will become abundant.

The last stage I'll talk about in marriage is the honeymoon and its first steps. We continue to build our love vocabulary. Love is intimacy. Intimacy is a shared identity, a 'we' relationship. It is like playing a stringed instrument. The music comes not from one string but from a combination of different strings and finger positions. We hear a lot about physical intimacy. This is important but God wants us to blend three loves into one. The physical, emotional and spiritual all are united in marriage. Couples have to learn to share emotional levels. The priority for women may be emotional and men physical. With a sensitive heart, we can experience each other's feelings. Barriers and walls must be lowered for intimacy to develop. We are fortunate the three blended loves have developed in our marriage union. The intimacy has enabled us to make life easier for one another instead of placing restrictive demands upon each other. We have been able to help each other become what God has designed us to become by nurturing each other through personal encouragement, inner strengthening and the establishment of peace and harmony between us. "Encourage one another and build each other up, just as in fact you are doing" (I Thess. 5:11).

No longer are we strangers. In our commitment, we have become transparent. Every day, until our exit from this earth into the heavens, we will be learning about each other. The Word of God indicates that the marriage commitment is both holy and practical. God used the marriage relationship to describe his relationship with the church, His Bride. He is committed to love unconditionally. Our marriage vows and covenant are very important to Him (Eph. 5:21-31; Rev. 22:17; Matt. 9:15). Our love is a pledge of mutual fidelity and mutual submission. It is an opportunity for each of us to grow and develop in our abilities and giftedness.

SIXTEEN

THE B.I.B.L.E
Psalm 107:2

The songwriter has written "The B-I-B-L-E, yes that's the book for me, I stand alone on the Word of God, the B-I-B-L-E." It shares the truth that "Jesus loves me, this I know, for the Bible tells me so." The medley ends with "There's one who stands before the Father's throne, He pleads for me, for I'm His Very Own, bought by His blood, so freely shed for me..." A little boy with blond hair and blue eyes would sing this medley to the glory of the Lord Jesus Christ. Our son, John, started singing when he was able to talk. He would share a Bible memory verse to introduce each medley of songs. Later his sister, Amy, would join him. In those early years, they would become the cover picture for a leaflet entitled, "The Music Room," an introduction to the importance of music in an individual's life. We had many good times in proclaiming the Word through music. I can't think of a time that they didn't join us in our church ministries.

John trusted his spirit, soul and body to Jesus Christ at an early age. I prayed with great intensity to be the one, along with his mother, to share the gospel with our son. This was my responsibility as his earthly father. The Holy Spirit led the way. It took place in the basement of our home in Comstock Park, a suburb of Grand Rapids. I can't remember the circumstance except it could have been one of those times we were working on a project together. Building projects were always exciting, but also a challenge because I am not a builder! Most everything that I try to build falls apart. I think John has increased in his abilities. He certainly didn't get the skills from me. As we worked, we talked. The conversation came around to Jesus Christ. I asked him if he would like Jesus to come into his heart and forgive his sins. I told him that Jesus loved him even more than I did. Jesus would like to take up residence in him. He knew the ABC's.

I translated the letters to biblical language. 'A' stands for admission. I have to admit that I don't measure up to God's standards. 'B' stands for belief. I have to believe what Jesus says that He loves me and gave His life on the cross to pay the penalty of sin. 'C' stands for confession. I have to agree with what Jesus said and did for me. These building blocks would hold together and not fall apart like our little projects. John learned that Christianity is progressive. Solid steps would be built as he grew in Jesus Christ day by day. This would happen through peer pressure, being a preacher's kid, living in a glass house, normal growing pains and learning Christ-like behavior.

He was identified with Jesus Christ in baptism along with some other youth from Central Lake who attended our church. This brought many questions, much decision making, many mistakes and some powerful experiences that would turn his life closer to Christ. This was not because dad wanted it but because the Holy Spirit allowed certain things to bring it about. God was faithful and will always be, through good and difficult times. I remember when John was around four or five years old that he caused quite a distraction in one of our services.

He always sat in the front row so Joy could sit with him when I preached. We were in the middle of an instrumental and vocal medley and I looked down at the first row. He was sitting in a theater-type seat and being small somehow his feet were the only parts of his body I could see. He had taken his socks and shoes off and I was afraid that he was on the way of removing some other clothes. It was hot that day. The teenage girls behind him were having a great time. I'll let you imagine what took place. Even though I was momentarily distracted, we ended up with a wonderful response in the service and the Holy Spirit helped us finish the service.

Without his physical birth, he would not experience a spiritual birth. John's birth was an answer to prayer as well. When she was a teenager, Joy would go to the stock car races with her brother. There was a lot of noise and anticipation. Would their favorite driver come in first? Who can go the fastest? Who can make the most damage? It was an exciting crowd and much energy could be released. In February of 1969, we could have used one of those drivers and a speedy car. We were expecting the arrival of our first child. I knew we would have a boy to start with because I requested it from God. I also wanted to have our family name continue into history as a testimony of God's grace. I was so positive on this matter that it caused some worry. I had to withdraw a little bit because Joy was concerned that if we didn't have a boy that I would be disappointed. When I realized that this was the case, I reassured her that, girl or boy, the child would be a gift from God and would be precious to me.

I was teaching at Lamont Christian School which was about thirty minutes away from our home. I was their first band instructor. We had a great time at the school. Practically everyone signed up for band. I was ready to leave the house and Joy yelled with an earnest voice, "I think you'd better stay home; we may be going to the hospital." I will always listen to her because she is usually right. Having been a nurse at the hospital, she wanted to wait as long as possible before going. This was really a poor decision. When it appeared that we had better leave, I could have used a race car driver. There has been only one time in my life that I would have appreciated a police escort. I prayed all the way to the hospital for a cop (used with respect) to stop me and then to lead the way to the emergency entrance.

I hit all the green lights on the way to the hospital. I kept praying that we would get there in time. I certainly didn't want to deliver a baby in the car. I kept telling Joy to relax and not to push which didn't seem to help very much. I am proud of her. With the new physical pain and emotional weariness, she really didn't have a lot of time to think. "It's happening!" she said. I jumped out of the car and got a wheelchair and yelled, "My wife is having a baby – now!" The nurse at the station and others rushed Joy away and told me she would be alright and to park the car. The nurse said that she was "crowning" and I wondered what that meant. I parked the car and was too late to see the baby born but, of course, in those days the father was not allowed to attend in the delivery room. I waited in the father's waiting room and another expectant father was pacing the floor. He asked me what my name was and I told him. He said, "Well they have been calling your name and said you just had a baby." Soon after that, the doctor came out and told me. I needed to know that Joy was alright and that the baby was okay and finally if God had answered my prayer for a baby boy.

We named our baby boy John. His name in Hebrew means "Yohanan" which means "Jehovah is gracious". The word "Jehovah" refers to God. In the Hebrew, YHWH is the name most frequently used for God. God is the Almighty, the great "I AM that I AM". The root idea is the concept of an existence without a beginning. He is independent. He has no need of us but loves us. He has no beginning or end. He is deity. The word gracious means that God has shown favor upon us. God's graciousness (favor, kindness, mercy) has been seen in our son's life. We called him John not only to carry our name into the future decades but to continue the flow of God's goodness in our lives. The Bible says in Psalm 107:2, "Let the redeemed of the Lord say so, whom He has redeemed from the hand of the enemy." Every testimony for Christ begins with a rescue followed by a thankful response. Psalm 107:1 says, "Oh, give thanks to the Lord, for He is good, for His mercy endures forever." John's journey has been one of rescue and of magnifying his Savior Jesus Christ.

John never learned to crawl like some kids. I remember hundreds of times I spent demonstrating what crawling looked like. I think he thought I was crazy. He never learned but I became a master at it. When he was about a year old, he went on his first journey. It was a short trip from the living room to the kitchen. Joy was baking some delicious food in the oven and John got too close to the oven door and lost his balance and fell against it. He put his hands out to catch himself and I tried to grab him but it wasn't soon enough to keep him from burning his hands. We were living in a little village and I was the only pastor in town. The entire village could have heard him cry. I ran to the village store to get something to take the sting away. I think the entire town thought we were abusive parents. I was thankful that Joy was a nurse and knew what to do. We all came through the ordeal alright. It wasn't the best way to be introduced to the town and by Sunday, everyone wanted to see his hands. His hands healed and it wasn't as bad as we thought but he had a big voice! God was gracious.

John had another incident in those early days. It was scary for him and for us, but God intervened. He woke up and couldn't open his eyelids because they were infected. Again, we were in a small town and didn't have the privilege of emergency services. We did find the help that we needed and his eyes cleared up. The fear turned to thanksgiving and the worry turned to confidence in God.

John has always been inquisitive and tries to figure things out. This is alright, but as parents this caused us some grief. I thought he might become a construction engineer. We moved into a new development area and our house was one of the first to be built. There were many lots and large and deep holes in the ground. We were inspecting our new home and discovered that John was missing. We called and called but no answer. We went out the sliding doors and saw some dog tracks. We started to search and finally heard a little voice far away. He had followed the dog and then decided to go down in the basement of the new houses being constructed. He was preparing a ladder to climb out and he probably would have made it out. We were relieved and so very glad to find him and to also see he was alright.

When John's sister came along and joined the family, he would play tricks on her. One day, he thought he would teach her a new way to get to the basement. I was downstairs and he thought he would take a short cut to see where I was. He was going to send Amy first but decided, like a big brother, that he should show her the way. He decided to go through the clothes chute. He put his head in the chute first to check things out but got stuck. Amy came running downstairs yelling, "dad-dad...look up." I thought that this might be a good sermon title "Look Up" but she meant to look up in the clothes chute. John's head was stuck. He couldn't move his head either way. For a moment, I thought we might have to call the fire department. We used soap and water on his head to work it out. We finally succeeded and what a delight it was to see his head still connected to his neck. There were no scars that time, but they would come later in his teens.

I was worship leader and music director at a church in Grand Rapids while studying and teaching. God's gracious act of kindness was shown to us again during a tornado. I was leading worship when an announcement was given to me. A tornado was heading our way so I quietly dismissed the congregation and told them to head toward the basement. My greatest concern was my family at home because they were in the direct line of the storm. The pastor took over and I called home from the church and told Joy what was happening. I told her to go to the neighbor's basement. I told her I would try to get home and would be careful. I took off and started to drive with my eyes glued to the sky with my mind on the family. It was very hot and humid and it started to rain and blow like crazy. When my car started to lift off the ground, I knew I was in trouble. The tornado left me and hit the ground a mile down the road from me. I arrived home safe in God's hands. The family members were afraid but John and Amy had their minds busy with the neighbor kids and Joy had the support she needed. When the tornado hit the ground, it did a lot of damage around us but our immediate area was spared.

The Lord gave John a bright mind. He would excel in his studies. He caught on quickly and was able to gain confidence. His elementary education laid the foundation for future studies. I made sure the studies met his needs. When I was in high school, I learned to study by having books around me. The room was quiet and I could concentrate. My grandfather built elaborate book shelves for my bedroom walls. They were my motivation. John was the direct opposite in his study habits. He would sit on the floor in the living room with TV on, CD's playing and conversations around and including him in the room. He would still accomplish an "A" for a grade. It takes both kinds of study habits. At the present time, he is working on his second Master's degree. Today he would say, "I have always enjoyed learning and, for the most part, love the process as well as the product of studying. I still think that if I could get paid for it, I would love to be a life-long graduate student." He would also include, "It is no coincidence that this was modeled in our home. I can still remember countless hours of studying and preparation by my dad that took place in his office, at the kitchen table or practicing a sermon while walking in the backyard."

John loves teaching and giving guidance to students. He has, over the years, made many student friendships. He is creative and I think anyone would obtain knowledge from his classes. He made history come alive. His teaching experiences developed an interest in counseling. Now he has many opportunities to assist the youth he is responsible for in changing their behavior and integrating God's way of thinking.

His coaching experiences have been highlights in his life journey. The teaching would be integrated into the gym. Every game became a learning opportunity for the students. He could handle winning and losing. Of course, winning would be much better but there was always something to learn. He always showed sensitivity to his team. He knew the rules of the game and how to produce them on the basketball court. He knew what it was like to get hurt. He played most of the sports in high school. When it came time to receive a varsity jacket, it was hard to decide what letter to put on it.

With his success came suffering. I remember the vomiting at a track meet, the fast balls in baseball nearly hitting him, the high speed run to the Traverse City hospital with an ankle injury even though he continued to play until the end of the game. There was a later injury to his knee causing an operation, braces, crutches and a cane. What a life of excitement and challenge. It all paid off. In college he would be able to go on a mission trip to beautiful Hawaii and hold basketball tournaments. What a great adventure that became witnessing for Jesus while playing basketball. This would lead to many overseas mission opportunities. God has been gracious.

As a family, we have spent many hours together having fun doing adventurous things, foolish things and just about anything you can think of like countless hours at church, being in the backyard, laughing, playing together, caring for our dogs and enjoying crazy travel trips. You can see through our experiences what priorities were in first place. When John left for college, it was very hard and yet at the same time encouraging and exciting. We relied on the Holy Spirit. I thought back to the time we sent him off on the school bus for his first time. This little, shy, cute, quiet, sensitive, smart boy has now grown up. We sent John off to college with a personal letter from us and a calm assurance that God would direct his life because through God's grace he had the right foundation to build upon. As a little boy sent off to school to kindergarten, he forgot to get off the bus at the designated stop and the driver didn't even realize that he still had a rider when he got back to the bus garage. We were waiting for him to get off the bus by the house and when he didn't, I immediately jumped in my car and followed the bus back to school. John wasn't alone because Jesus was with him. He seemed to be alright when we got him off the bus. I did have a little chat with the driver.

In 2006, John shared "from early childhood to the present day, the concept of absolute truth has been instilled in me by my parents and grandparents. Everything about our family, although not perfect, was based in part or in whole on our faith in Jesus Christ. Those values of hard-working commitment, honor, integrity, faithfulness, sensitivity, unconditional love, selflessness, etc. were modeled for me and they hopefully will continue to the next generation of Gillette's through my identity, through my ability to commit, through my being a faithful husband, in being a godly dad, in being a loyal friend, and in reaching out to others in love, etc."

SEVENTEEN

GLORIFY THY NAME
John 12:28

The songwriter has written, "Father, we love you, we worship and adore you, glorify thy name in all the earth." This is more than a song; it's Scripture, "Father, glorify your name" (John 12:28). It is a song and Scripture that our daughter Amy Joy would follow in her life. Does she have any other favorites? I'm sure she could pick out a few that have enabled her but she would say the entire Bible is her footstool to rely upon. Can a little child trust in Jesus? I suppose there could be a lot of discussion on that subject. I know, through the testimony of Amy, that a four-year-old can commit her spirit, soul and body to Jesus Christ. Her mother and I were there as her witnesses. I told her that Jesus loved her and wanted to be a part of her life. I called it the "double A plan". All she had to do was believe in what Jesus said about Himself. She knew John 3:16, "For God so loved the world that He gave His only begotten son, that whosoever believeth in Him should not perish but have everlasting life." God loves her and created her to know Him personally. When I said God, she understood who I was talking about. She understood through the things she could see, touch feel and His Word.

God wanted a relationship with her. The first "A" refers to acknowledging the need. She knows what a fatherly relationship is about because she has a father that loves her and cares for her. She knew also that to meet God's standards she would have to accept Jesus Christ as her Savior. This was the second "A" in the plan. To do this was not a hard thing for her to do. She said, "Jesus loves me and gave His life on a cruel cross to pay the price for my sin", understanding that sin means missing the mark. His standard can only be accomplished through Jesus Christ.

She accepted Him by believing and praying Him into her heart. She said that "it is like drinking a glass of milk." She had some milk and cookies that evening before she went to bed. She has been drinking His Word since that day into her life. Today she would say that Christianity is progressive. It involves dynamic discipleship. She wrote a note to me that proves that a four year old's decision with parental prayer and growth in grace means something. On a father's day card from 2007 she wrote, "Big D...thanks dad for always believing in me, loving me and trusting me. Thanks also for teaching by example how to trust God with my goals and desires and believing in the impossible. You've taught me how to dream big and take risks... love you always."

Her life has been an adventure in faith. Here are a few highlights that reveal her growth and ours in God's grace. It all began with her birth. We named her Amy Joy because it means beloved. She would certainly be loved. She was a gift from God, a perfect, beautiful gift of joy. Her second name is her mother's name. We have always wanted our children to carry our names into the next generation and continue sharing the grace of our Lord Jesus Christ. Without a doubt, our strategy in bringing her into this world would not be the same as our son's. Because his entrance was sudden - we hardly made it to the hospital in time - a little bit more planning would be just fine. We had to prepare for her brother's care when this child arrived. It was good to have grandparents that we could trust and rely on. I was pastor of a church at this time. Everything was in order – schedules, duties, details of life. John was born at 4:00 pm with the rush of the city around us. Amy would be born at 4:00 am in the quietness of the early hours.

We were blessed once again. I counted her fingers and toes and everything was in place. We witnessed a true genuine miracle. What a humble privilege to be given this gift. God answered our prayers. I knew we would have a little girl come into our home. This would make our home perfect. A boy and a girl would make it complete. Now, after so many years, I think Joy and I wouldn't mind having a dozen or so more children. In a way, because of my teaching, we have had the opportunity to share with many children. Someday, I'll count them all. There is nothing more exciting than to have the children around. Of course, now we get tired faster and when nap time comes, guess who gets to take the nap?

Joy seemed to handle the delivery of Amy Joy alright. It was strange again to be left out of the delivery room. I have had to miss those crucial times. Hospital rules kept me from assisting my wife. I think I would have done well. The doctor once again gave me the news. After giving Joy some rest, I picked up John from grandma's house. He was so excited when seeing his sister. As a matter of fact, he wanted to hold her and was hugging her so tight that I had to tell him that she wasn't a doll, but she was alive and needed to breathe.

I have ministered to couples who have lost their babies through death and who have been challenged by disability. I have also witnessed God's love and grace in difficult times and happy times. Either way, God has shown His gracious presence. I am so glad that we have a heavenly Father that we can turn to through Jesus Christ. Tears of happiness or sadness will both bring rest and contentment.

We were glad to get back into routine. Joy was able to stay home in the early months after birth. Young John kept trying to teach Amy something or to tease her. I don't think that duo of actions has every stopped. Today they have high regard for each other and continue as great friends. A week hasn't gone by without communication between them. We have had our hands full with the two children and with both Joy and myself working. I was working on a double Bachelor's degree. Joy has earned the right to my degrees as much as I have. Happiness, joy, gratitude, thanksgiving and appreciation are words that mean something to us. The witness of Amy Joy's physical and spiritual births were the foundations of many more exciting acts of faith.

Amy trusted in Jesus Christ at the age of four. She had an opportunity to put that initial faith into daily practice. We traveled to Canada to speak at the Blue Water Bible Conference. It was our first family life conference and it was a beautiful place with horseback riding and swimming in the pool. We marveled while gazing into the pure blue sky above that matched the clear blue waters below. Amy was a quiet, timid, reserved, cute little girl. If she had been outspoken and liked public performance and attention, it would have been easier. She started early in her life realizing that God will listen to her and help her to do whatever she had to do. She would pray, "Help me Jesus if I'm in the water playing or on the platform with dad or mom." She learned to talk to Jesus as if she was talking to her friends or parents. The time to make a Jesus relationship real is at childhood. You learn to take Jesus at His Word and believe it. She did that and this trusting faith has followed her along in life. This doesn't mean that it has been easy but the sovereign God has been with her.

When she entered preschool at Northland Baptist Church, she became the cover girl for their advertisement. This experience brought new "trusting in Jesus" prayers. She would learn to entrust her day to the Lord. The new friends, new teachers, other adult helpers would be people to adjust to. Slowly and with caution, she would begin to open up. Years later, she would be on the cover of a college advertisement. We would see the little girl grow into a God-honoring young woman. Leadership would spring forth through Bible study groups and social committees.

When we moved from Grand Rapids to Torch Lake to minister, it was another step of faith and growth. Making friends in preschool and elementary grades was difficult at times but entering junior high school would be something much bigger. She prayed that the Lord would bring somebody across her path that was more nervous, more afraid and scared than herself. The Lord answered her prayer with a girl with the same first name, Amy. They met on the front steps of the school as they entered to enroll. That was a wonderful lift of confidence and security. They would continue their friendship through the years.

Amy tried her hand at playing the flute in band but would prefer percussion. She ended up having a problem with the flute because of the acid in her system causing a problem with the silver on the instrument. She was encouraged to try out for the girl's soft ball team. She didn't do well with sports even though she looked great in the uniform.

When she entered high school, she found a career in cheerleading. She would learn patience, endurance and steadfastness in those years. She could learn the cheerleading routine early. If it was for football or basketball, it was always a fun time. Competition was heavy, teen girl socializing was challenging, boy problems arose, and her brother was liked by girls in her class. During those years there were many lunch break visits or after school vocal encouragements.

It was fun as parents to watch both of them on the gym floor, John as a basketball player and Amy as a cheerleader.

I remember many experiences that happened in Amy's life. I will mention only two here that have encouraged me personally at times of need. After a busy Sunday in ministry, Monday rolled in and I was ready to study and prepare. Research and study have always been a delight for me. After lunch, I was sitting in the backyard and Amy joined me. I asked her if she had learned anything from my sermon the previous day. She looked straight at me and said, "No". I was a bit surprised but not shocked. I asked her why? Then an afternoon of discussion took place and it was very good. I put some of her ideas into action. She was being an encourager. As a teenager, she needed to have something to grab hold of in her heart. The next Monday, I asked her again about the preaching and I had improved. I have always tried to improve. Preachers need to be able to communicate. Sometimes I have wondered if my personal family has been nurtured. Then I look at the content of the message and the Holy Spirit's leading and I leave it in His hands.

The second experience happened just before her graduation year. The previous few years were extremely busy. You can get a feel for them in reading my booklet "Triple Torch." This was written for my 50th anniversary in proclaiming the Word through music education, pastoring and para church ministries. I was preaching my sermons for Sunday. After studying, I would preach through the sermons each day through the week. The Holy Spirit would give me new insights for the message. It would become second nature to my own life. I should live it out before I challenge my congregation with it. I was standing by the pulpit and I could imagine the people in their favorite seats. I cannot remember what point I was on but suddenly I had a lot of pain, and it was nothing like I have experienced before. It was sharp and heavy at the same time in the back, shoulders, arms, and chest. I dropped my Bible and fell down to the floor. "What is happening to me," I thought, not out loud because I couldn't speak. I prayed "I don't want to leave my family" but then it got so severe I just cried out for help. A little later I was able to get home which was next door to the church. Joy and I made a trip to the hospital. I went through a lot of testing and the doctors determined that I had a silent heart attack. We kept a low key with this experience. There are a lot of things that could be shared but Amy sent a note of encouragement which helped me through this experience.

In Amy's life, she has always been able to find cards that make people think and laugh and even cry all at the same time. She knew that I was a lover of dogs. We certainly have had several in our family relations, little and big, dumb and smart, but always needing attention and a close friend. The picture on the card was an oversized nose of a dog placed on the body of a little dog. There were some crazy words with the picture. This caused a relaxed mindset that was needed, as I was going through this unknown physical testing. She would always include some spiritual remarks. She reminded me of what I have taught her. Faith is a decision to trust in the words of a sovereign God who has our best interest in mind. Faith when activated develops patience. I had to learn to let go of self and learn to hold onto someone that can do whatever He pleases. Waiting for God's response is always the best way to go. When you rehearse all of His attributes, they produce peace. I needed to be reminded that I was not alone. I know this and Joy does also, but it was encouraging to have our daughter remind us of this fact.

Amy knows what God wants for her in a love and marriage relationship. It's a love produced from a pure single heart, not divided. A pure heart wills what God wills no matter what the cost. It's not a faint, confused, ignorant, liberal or uncommitted heart. Love is the balance of physical attraction, social companionship and spiritual union. It is a love that is demonstrated through having patience and looks for a way of being constructive. It is not possessive and not anxious to impress nor does it cherish ideas of its own importance.

Love has good manners and does not pursue selfish advantage. It is not touchy and it does not keep an account of evil or gloat over the weakness of other people. It is glad when truth prevails. Love knows no limit to its endurance, no end to its trust, and no fading of its hope. It can outlast anything and is, in fact, the one thing that still stands when all else has fallen (I Cor. 13:4-8 Phillips). It knows how to answer the question, should you marry someone who loves you deeply or should you marry someone you love deeply? The answer is both.

Amy has been called to live by faith. Everything that happens, God's Word tells us, fits into a pattern for good to those who love Him. The more intimately we walk with Him, the more faithfully we trust His promises and keep His commandments, the simpler and the happier we will be. Life will un-complicate itself. She knows what it is like to have a broken heart. "The Lord is close to the brokenhearted and saves those who are crushed in spirit" (Psalm 34:18). In her engagement circumstance, she would find God's grace and lay hold of His power to recreate, to redeem, to forgive and to mend. Hearts do break but God is in sovereign control of our lives and of every single thing that touches them. Nothing harmful can pass through the fortress of His love. He has a glorious purpose in permitting the heartbreak. She discovered many insights from her situation; sufferings are not in vain. Over the years, she would examine Romans 8:29 and she would come to trust (2 Cor. 1:8-9), to obey (Psalm 119:67, 71), to bear fruit (John 15:2), and to strive for spiritual maturity (James 1:4). A broken heart is an acceptable offering to God. Can we imagine the good He can bring through her simple offering? The trial of faith is a thing worth much more than gold.

Her testimony today is found in Psalm 38:9-10, 15, "I wait for you, O Lord, you will answer, O Lord my God." He always answers the cry of one who wills, against all wanting, to do His will. His will is to glorify him if single or married.

Psalm 37:5-6 says, "Commit your way to the Lord; trust in Him and He will do this: He will make your righteousness shine like the dawn, the justice of your cause like the noonday sun." Commitment entails the acceptance of responsibility. It imposes a task and a trust. It is a promise to do something. Amy, our daughter, has committed herself to the Lord Jesus Christ in whom she loves.

Amy has worked successfully with two mega-churches. She was thrown into supernatural activities at Mars Hill Bible Church as their first administrative assistant. She was able to witness a blast from 600 to 6,000 attendees in only a few months. She leaped into a daily organizing routine for the church offices. She was able to witness regular opportunities of God's intervention. She learned through her love for Jesus that she could have personal control when faced with unexpected issues. She learned how to be gentle and firm with disturbed church members in need. Meekness and goodness have been demonstrated to her teen girls' Bible study group through her submission to Jesus. He is big enough to care for anything that comes up in life. God has the answers to the multiple problems of growing up. She has been a vessel being used, sometimes to fill the gap between parent and child.

At Calvary Church, she put the same promises into action. She learned much through the leadership in worship and outreach ministries. She discovered gifts she didn't know she had. At present, she is ministering at a multi-ethnic church. Tabernacle Community Church is a growing, exciting ministry that the Holy Spirit is developing. It's a real ride toward the future for her to continue the use of her gifts.

When Amy was a little girl, I would go on visitation calls to many homes. Sometimes I would go alone, sometimes Joy would join me and at other times the children would travel with me. We were visiting one of our elderly couples in their home. They had been in the kitchen so we joined them and sat down for a little while to visit. They were taking some medicine and Amy thought it was pretty amazing to see so many pills on the table. She wanted to know what ailment the pills were for and how they would help the ailment. There were big ones and little ones and she counted at least a dozen for each person. We had a good discussion on God's creation and how our bodies lose some of their energy and function with age. Then out of the blue, she said to me, "Why don't you give them a pastoral prescription? A medical doctor has given them all those pills for their body, you're a doctor of the soul, why not give them a prescription from God?" It was a good idea. A prescription for peace and endurance was given and the "pastoral prescriptions" have continued to be given out since that time. Amy has been able to live with peace in her life because she has a close love relationship with God through Jesus Christ. Her decisions have been made with tranquility and a quiet spirit because she loves, adores, worships and glorifies her Lord and Savior Jesus Christ.

EIGHTEEN

JESUS IS THE SWEETEST NAME I KNOW
Psalm 39:7, 12

The songwriter has written, "Jesus is the sweetest name I know and He's just the same as His lovely name, and that's the reason why I love Him so, O Jesus is the sweetest name I know." Sometimes life is cruel, sometimes it is full of suffering, physically and psychologically, sometimes our life expectations fail, sometimes there is little meaning to life, sometimes there is desperation and despair and sometimes there is just a falling-out in the realities of life. Hope in the Scripture is always a confident expectation. The Word carries with it no uncertainties. I can be sure of the faithfulness of God in fulfilling His promises. With hope, I have conviction and assurance. I want to become contagious with encouragement and endurance that springs from hope. Hope is the answer.

People with long-standing problems need hope. People with peculiarly difficult problems need hope. People that have been misled in regards to their problems need hope. People who are harassed by fear need hope. People whose hopes have been dashed repeatedly need hope. People that have tried and failed need hope. People that have dramatic changes in life need hope. People that have fallen into depression need hope. People who have suffered life shattering experiences need hope.

When I find myself searching for help, I find it in the hope that I have in Jesus. I have learned through Psalm 39:1-13 my innermost thoughts toward the wicked should be confident and not complaining. I should not embarrass God with my tongue (v.1-2). My innermost thoughts toward God should be honest and not with a bitter attitude. I must share my anguish and pain (v.3-4). When I am searching for hope, my innermost thoughts toward myself should not be deceived. I have to learn God's perspective on life (v.5-6). My innermost thoughts toward deliverance should be Scripture-directed (v.7-13). I have learned that in despair, I can experience confidence (v.7). I have learned that in confession I can be released (v.8). I have learned that correction is needed sometimes (v.9-11). I have been comforted (v.12-13). These thoughts have started the path to hope.

I am discovering with excitement that in Jesus Christ's name, I can live with hope and obtain the help I need. He is worth believing. There is no one whose understanding of life has come close to His. Jesus is in the life changing business. All kinds of people have come to Him: satisfied people, messed-up people, sick people, injured people, forgotten people, despised people, admired people, worthy people and religious people. I have come to Him. Jesus has been changing lives for two thousand years. I am learning to leap out of my skin into faith. It is a realization that there must be less of me and more of Him. Not only do I have to let go of self and replace self with Him, but I have to learn to wait. This is the in-between period. When I hold onto His promise, "My hope is in Jesus...hear my prayer, O Lord, listen to my cry for help" (Psalm 39:7, 12). I know victory will come because He keeps to his word. Some adjustments have to be made during the waiting time for victory.

As I apply the attributes of God to the names given to Jesus, I will be given help and hope.

His name is wonderful (Isaiah 9:6). I believe in an awesome God. He can make my life wonderful because He is wonderful. My first adjustment in obtaining help is believing that He is awesome. Wonderful things have happened, are happening and will continue to happen. It all starts with experiencing forgiveness of sin and the invasion of a whole new life. "Christ liveth in me" (Galatians 2:20). Believing in Jesus is required (Acts 16:31). He wants intimate fellowship. "I count all things to be loss in view of the surpassing value of knowing Christ Jesus my Lord" (Philippians 3:7-8). Knowing God is the most important thing I can accomplish. My goal is to know Him so well that I can say, "I have received a spirit of adoption as sons by which I cry, 'Abba! Father!'" The word 'Abba' is an equivalent of daddy. It is a term of respect and endearment.

As a continuation of this first adjustment, I can better understand how I am to live by truly knowing God. As I contemplate God's attributes through His names, I have been promised strength, encouragement and help. I know God loves me. God is love and the one who abides in love abides in God and God abides in him (I John 4:16). I am surrounded with his infinite person, power and glory (John 14:20). "And I will pray the Father, and He shall give you another comforter, that He may abide with you forever…I am in my Father, and ye in me, and I in you" (v.16, 20). He says, "I am in you." He is more than with me, He is *in* me. He also supplies in Himself all that any soul will ever need in time or for eternity. The union I have 'in Christ' is beyond my comprehension. The oneness that I have with Jesus means many things (John 17:20-23). My emphasis here is fellowship. It is awesome to say that I have an everlasting companionship with Him; in the place we live He abides. I am looking for the eternal security which starts here and now as I draw near to Him. "To be in Christ" refers to my position, my union, with Christ. In believing, I have that relationship and possession of the divine. I am safe in His hands because I am associated with the creator-redeemer God. "Christ in me" refers to transformation power.

His name is counselor. I believe in an all-knowing God. He is my counselor. He knows everything. "Who has directed the Spirit of the Lord or as His counselor has informed Him? With whom did He consult and gave Him understanding? And who taught Him in the path of justice and taught Him knowledge, and informed Him of the way of understanding?" (Isaiah 40:13-14). God knows what He knows simply because He knows it. He did not learn it. The second adjustment is to accept His counsel. He is qualified to counsel me. He is eternal God in whom "dwelleth all the fullness of the Godhead bodily" (Colossians 2:9). Jesus Christ was a part of the eternal counsel of creation. He was there when the Father said, "Let us make man." He understands me because He became man. He is able to enter into the experiences that perplex and burden me. He knows my heart and mind. He is able to help me understand myself. I have to let go of myself and let Him take over. I must sit back and learn to watch Him work. He knows me, my feelings, my desires, my personality and my disease. He has known everything from the beginning (Acts 15:18). Nothing can escape His all-encompassing knowledge. I have learned that God permits trials for reasons we may or may not understand, but He is able to bring good out of the worst circumstances. I am able to have confidence because He knows all the possibilities. He is personal. The Bible says, "O Lord, thou hast searched me and known me" (Psalm 139:1-2). He knows my thought process (Ezekiel 11:5). God is concerned about the details; He knows everything going on behind the scenes (Job 23:10).

His name is mighty God. I believe in a powerful God. Jesus is God himself. There is nothing God cannot do. His unlimited power will reflect His divine glory and accomplish His sovereign will. "Power belongs to God" (Psalm 62:11). He is able to "call into being that which does not exist" (Romans 4:17). "He spoke and it was done" (Psalm 33:6). Nothing is impossible with God (Luke 1:37). The Scripture says, "Thou hast formed my inward parts...I am fearfully and wonderfully made" (Psalm 139:13-14). God's power is very personal. "Thy will be done" (Matthew 5) is my prayer. He is able to deliver (Daniel 3:17). He is able to keep me standing in His presence (Jude 24). He says to be strong in the Lord and in the strength of his might (Ephesians 6:10). The third adjustment for change is embracing the fact that He is "mighty God." He is called "Immanuel" God with us. I have to understand His claims and accept His deity. With that response, I am strengthened with all might. He takes care of the demands of life. No matter what the problem He has power to meet it, handle it, solve it, and use it for my good and for His glory.

His name is everlasting Father. I believe in a sovereign God. He is the originator of eternity. I live in a new dimension of life. God has absolute rule and control over all of His creation. God rules absolutely over the affairs of men. God can do whatever He wants to do simply because it is all His. "The earth is the Lord's and all it contains, the world, and those who dwell in it" (Psalm 24:1). Everything that occurs does so under the hand of a sovereign God. The fourth adjustment for change is reveling in His name, the everlasting Father. God has created me for eternity and Jesus Christ came to earth to reveal eternity (I John 1:1, 2). There is more to life than what my senses reveal. In trusting Jesus, I am able to meet every detail of life with confidence. I am safe in Jesus because of who He is. I exist for Him. I can live in confidence because Jesus provides strength. There are no chance happenings. Whatever happens, it will bring good (Psalm 8:28). He has the whole picture. I can trust in Jesus and He is able to guard what I have entrusted to Him (2 Timothy 1:12).

His name is Prince of Peace. I believe in an intimate God. The fifth adjustment for change is peace. When I accomplish the alignment process through His grace, I will experience peace. Jesus brings peace because He is peace. Do not try to change the circumstances but change in character. Peace does not come from the outside in but in reality comes from the inside out. I am learning that my testing, trials and temptations can become a win-win situation. I must learn to let go of self. I must learn to make the adjustments. I must learn to practice the victory in peace. He is free from limitations of space. He is everywhere present. He is in me (I John 4:4). I believe in an awesome God because He is wonderful in all His acts. He wants fellowship with me. I believe in an all-knowing God because He provides wise counsel. He has all knowledge. He knows my inner needs. I believe in a powerful God because there is nothing He cannot do. I believe in a sovereign God because He is the originator of eternity. He is in control. When I reflect upon these facts and allow them to penetrate my spirit, soul and body, I am able to face today.

As I repeat the names of Jesus with a sincere

heart and allow the Holy Spirit to enable me, I will be encouraged. This is a starting point. Authentic transformation takes time; it is a process. It is not a formula to follow; it is not a list of basic principles to apply. It is not a mechanical determination. It is faith working in me through the Holy Spirit's guidance and power. "May the God of hope fill you with all joy and peace as you trust in Him, so that you may overflow with hope by the power of the Holy Spirit" (Romans 15:13).

The promise of help is provided through Jesus. I am thankful for the Lord's presence. This chapter was written when I started a new journey in my life. I am facing a fearful, dreadful uncertainty in my health. The biopsy has returned with a positive result. Cancer is the disease. I was told that my cancer is the second killer of man. That information was really discouraging. I am waiting for the details and what treatment options I have. I can list some of them but do not like the side effects. I still need to know the facts. The initial shock has started to wear off. My family is very supportive. I know their prayers and spiritual perspective will continue to be helpful.

My daughter shared a prayer and Psalm 91:11,

which says, "He who dwells in the shelter of the Most High will rest in the shadow of the Almighty." She has started a network of prayer support. My son immediately gave me a verse from Hosea 6:3, "Let us acknowledge the Lord…as surely as the sun rises He will appear…He will come to us." He has also set up a network of prayer warriors. I am so pleased that they have accepted this challenge in the way that they have. They know what works and they know what pleases God. Both Bible references, without them knowing it, reinforce the verse the Holy Spirit gave to me and my wife, James 4:8, "Draw near to God and he will draw near to you." My dark thoughts have turned to the light because Jesus is wonderful. My folly has turned to wise thinking because Jesus is my counselor. Losing heart has changed to a conquering spirit because Jesus is my mighty God. I have been drawing closer to my everlasting Father who holds eternity in His hands. When I think of these names of Jesus, peace from the Prince of Peace has entered my spirit. "Jesus is the sweetest name I know and He's just the same as His lovely name, and that's the reason why I love Him so, O Jesus is the sweetest name I know."

NINETEEN

WE SHALL BEHOLD HIM
Psalm 27:4, 5, 8

The songwriter has written, "The sky shall unfold, preparing His entrance, the stars shall applaud Him with thunders of praise and we shall behold Him." "One thing I ask of the Lord that I may dwell in the house of the Lord all the days of my life, to gaze upon the beauty of the Lord and to seek Him in His temple. For in the day of trouble, He will keep me safe…my heart says of you, seek His face! Your face, Lord, I will seek" (Psalm 27:4, 5, 8). This means with intensity. In the previous verses, a strong affirmation of confidence has been recorded. "The Lord is my light and my salvation, whom shall I fear" (v.1-3). The New Testament counterpart to this is "If God be for us, who can be against us" (Romans 8:31). My life is and will continue to be wrapped with His arms (v.4-5). I will have a sense of His protection and will not worry but music will flow into my heart (v.6).

Some people think that Jesus was just God. Some people think that He was just man, and some people say that Jesus was an angel. Some think that He was an angel and man. I believe that Jesus was and is God incarnate which means that He is both God and man. Jesus was born of a human mother (Galatians 4:4). He grew up like any other human being (Luke 2:52). He was hungry (Matthew 4:4) and thirsty (John 19:28). He grew weary and needed rest (John 4:6). He felt sadness and cried (John 11:3335). He suffered (John 19:1), died (John 19:33) and was buried (John 19:40-42). He was human in every sense that we are, yet He was without sin (Hebrews 4:15).

I have discovered that He is one person who has two natures, human and divine. Jesus, God the Son, existing as the second person of the triune God, united His divine nature to a human nature, and through that came into the world. He did not stop being God when He added humanity to Himself. Remember,

God has no limitations. We are "one-dimensional beings" and He is not. In Deuteronomy 6:4, it says "Yahweh, our God; Yahweh is a plurality within an indivisible unity." God is one divine nature shared by three persons – the Father, Son and Holy Spirit. God the Son having an infinite nature assumed in addition a finite nature. There is one divine nature or essence of God. In Jesus Christ, we have added a human nature. Jesus is the Son of God (Lord) and Son of Man (Savior).

The miracles in prophecy give evidence to his claims. Consider the following:

• The Christ (Messiah) will be born of a woman (Genesis 3:15).

• He will be born of a virgin (Isaiah 7:14). •He will be of the seed of Abraham (Genesis 12:1-3; 22:18).

• He will be of the tribe of Judah (Genesis 49:10; Luke 3:23,33).

• He will be of the House of David (2 Samuel 7:12; Matthew 1:1).

• His birthplace will be Bethlehem (Micah 5:2; Matthew 2:1).

• He will be anointed by the Holy Spirit (Isaiah 11:2; Matthew 3:16-17).

- He will be heralded by a messenger of God (Isaiah 40:3; Matthew 3:1-2).

- He will perform miracles (Isaiah 35:5-6; Matthew 9:35).

- He will cleanse the temple (Malachi 3:1; Matthew 21:12).

- He will be rejected by his own people (Psalm 118:22; I Peter 2:7).

- He will die some 483 years after 444b.c. (Daniel 9:24).

- He will die a humiliating death (Psalm 22; Isaiah 53; Matthew 27) involving: Rejection by Israel (Isaiah 53:3; John 1:10-11; 7:5, 48). Silence before his accusers (Isaiah 53:7; Matthew 27:12-19). Humiliation – being mocked (Psalm 22:7-8; Matthew 27:31). Piercing of his hands and feet (Psalm 22:16; John 20:25). Being crucified with thieves (Isaiah 53:12; Luke 23:33). Praying for his persecutors (Isaiah 53:12; Luke 23:34). Piercing of his side (Zechariah 12:10; John 19:34). Burial in a rich man's tomb (Isaiah 53:9; Matthew 27:57-60). Casting lots for his garments (Psalm 22:18; John 19:23-24).

- He will rise from the dead (Psalm 16:10; March 16:6; Acts 2:31).

- He will ascend into heaven (Psalm 68:18; Acts 1:9).

- He will sit at the right hand of God (Psalm 110:1; Hebrews 1:3).

All these and many more prophecies (nearly two hundred) were fulfilled in the person of Jesus of Nazareth who claimed to be "the Christ, the Son of God" (Matthew 26:63-64).

His life gives evidence to his divine nature. His life was miraculous from the beginning. Here are the acts of God to prove it:

- He was born of a virgin (Matthew 1:21; Luke 1:27).

- He turned water into wine (John 2:7).

- He walked on water (Matthew 14:25). •He multiplied bread (John 6:11).

- He opened the eyes of the blind (John 9:7).

- He made the lame walk (Mark 2:3). •He cast out demons (Mark 1:34).

- He healed the multitudes of all kinds of sickness (Matthew 9:35).

- He raised the dead to life (John 11:43-44).

- He knew what men were thinking in their hearts (John 2:25).

His sinless life gives evidence of His divine nature. From the lips of Jesus' most intimate friends and disciples who had lived with Him for several years at close range we receive glowing testimonies:

- Peter – "A lamb without blemish or defect" (I Peter 1:19)
- Paul – He 'had no sin" (2 Corinthians 5:21)
- Author of Hebrews – "…yet was without sin" (Hebrews 4:15)
- John – "He is pure" (I John 3:3)
- Jesus – "Can any of you prove me guilty of sin?" (John 8:46) (Jesus directed this question to those looking for a reason to convict Him.)

The most critical act of God was Jesus' resurrection from the dead. The fact that both the Old Testament and Jesus predicted in advance that He would rise from the dead makes the miracle that much more powerful.

- "You will not abandon me to the grave, nor will you let your Holy One see decay" (Psalm 16:10).
- The Messiah will come and die (Isaiah 53; Psalm 22).
- The Messiah will have an enduring political reign from Jerusalem (Isaiah 9:6; Daniel 2:44). (For

the Messiah to die, then reign, He would have to rise from the dead.)

- "Destroy this temple of Jesus' body, and I will raise it again in three days" (John 2:19-21).
- "For as Jonah was three days and three nights in the belly of a huge fish, so the Son of man will be three days and three nights in the heart of the earth" (Matthew 12:30).
- "The Son of man must suffer…and He must be killed and on the third day be raised to life" (Luke 9:22).
- "No one takes my life from me, but I lay it down of my own accord, I have authority to lay it down and authority to take it up again" (John 10:18).

I have looked at His true identity, through studying and observing the Biblical accounts of the miracles in prophecy, the miracles in His life, His sinless life, the testimony of close witnesses and His resurrection. The evidence is there to be believed, but as Jesus said, "If they do not listen to Moses and the prophets, they will not be convinced even if someone rises from the dead" (Luke 16:31). I am convinced that Jesus Christ can do whatever He wills to do according to His character. Jesus is my spiritual and physical healer. Whatever my needs are, He already knows about them. He knows how I will react or act toward them. He knows what works for me. He knows what is best for me. My decision is simply, "Thy will be done." My responsibility is to gaze upon Jesus intently. In my intense search, He will make me free in my need. He said, "If you remain in my word, you are truly my disciples and you will know the truth and the truth will make you free" (John 8:31, 32).

I have confidence in Him because of who He is. If I learn to do what He says to do, I will have continual assurance of His presence, power and peace. These characteristics will be flowing through my veins because I have learned to take His perspective in all things. Real hope for me is freedom and growth found in God's grace. Everything I have been writing about seems to be a mystery. It works if I gaze upon Jesus and obey His Word. The Scripture starts with "If you…" I must respond with my head and heart to the gospel. In my childhood, I received Jesus into my life and began a growing relationship. The Christian walk is hard and can be a struggle because the old nature is fighting against it. I have and will continue to relinquish my will to Jesus because true liberation comes when my heart says" yes" to God's words "follow me."

I carry in my billfold a pastoral prescription card. It refreshes my mind to do certain things if I want freedom. Many things can go wrong and bring pain, confusion, worry and struggle, health, finances, addictions, motives, decisions, self-esteem, confidence, etc. As I continually gaze upon Jesus, I will be set free. The prescription offers a Biblical solution. It is an "exchange strategy" (Philippians 4:6-9). I am learning to recite appropriate Scripture to meet my need. His perspectives, with prayer and thanksgiving, replace mine. Reflection follows with His presence providing reason for praise and positive memories. This will lead to reliance on His promises which becomes a habitual meditation. Thinking right becomes an ordinary practice. His perspective, His presence, His promises and His power take over in my life pattern and bring peace and a single focus. Jesus is indeed my healer.

TWENTY

FOLLOW, I WILL FOLLOW THEE
Psalm 19:7, 8

The songwriter has written, "Jesus calls me – I must follow, follow Him today, when His tender voice is pleading, how can I delay?" I know the blessing of His presence. I have experienced His power. I will follow Him every passing day. My journey has been successful because the Bible has brought success. As I travel back and forth in reading and re-reading *Discovering God's Favor*, it has demonstrated that Holy Scripture is the book to follow and that it will achieve what it wants to achieve. I love the promise in Proverbs 21:21, "He that followeth after righteousness and mercy findeth life, righteousness and honor." It is not a matter of trying to be successful.

Failure doesn't create discouragement either. The Bible says very clearly that it provides confidence because it produces its own success. I cannot stand and give honor to myself. I can only bow before a Holy God in worship and humility. He prepares the way and pushes me in it. We will face wars with the enemy and it is hard because he is invisible. He is a trained specialist in deceit. In all the transitions of my life, God's Word has given victory. I have written devotionals on God's sovereignty, His creation and salvation, and through His Word, my own heart changed. It wasn't an intellectual accent to the gospel. I have written about my own alternative syndrome, death, communion with God and how His Word has brought relational steadfastness.

I even wrote about pre-adolescence and my teen years. Words like trust, commitment, submission, respect, resolve and sincerity play an important part in those years. It all was real because of His Word. I have been thankful and will continue to thank God for His spiritual insight and sovereignly bestowed spiritual awakening. I realize that many things I have tried to teach have been taught already. Maybe remembrance is what is important. I have, through the years, been taught many principles. For them to work in my life, I need to practice and remember them. I have spent time writing about why I believe in the Bible. I have written about my pastoral/ministerial, educational/musical and para-church ministries. Through discipleship in God's Word, each ministry has been grounded. His Word has been the foundation to my ministry in music education. I belong to a teaching staff, do some tutoring and consultation. It has all been possible through God's providential Word. Building relationships and sharing the Word have been a blessing. The subjects of love and marriage, parental guidance and pastoral ministry insights have increased my confidence in God's Word because it brings results. The Word has brought me into interaction with God. Communication with our Father has brought immeasurable blessing. The promises of God have been a safety net encircling my life. It is exciting to read what the Bible says about itself. It is more exciting to put it into action.

Notice what it says in Psalm 19:7, "The law of the Lord is perfect, converting the soul." When I see the word 'law' I think of Moses. His statue can be seen in Washington DC as "the great law giver." The law statement takes in the entire doctrine of God. The whole body of scriptural truth is found in the Bible. It is perfect because it is the testimony of God. It converts the soul. It brings restoration. This begins with faith in Jesus Christ which was accomplished in my life as a child. I simply took God at His Word and believed in Christ's death and resurrection for my deliverance. This has developed into a lifelong process of transformation (Romans 12:2). This caused a change in my inward nature. My mind, the center of logical reasoning, ethical judgment and moral awareness, was changed. It has become Christ-centered, not through my will but through God's transforming power. The Word has changed my life from the inside out. It all started in my childhood, praise God!

"The testimony of the Lord is sure, making wise the simple" (Psalm 19:7b). This is a declaration of truth and a statement of fact. It is a witness of God's story and is the precept that God wants us to know. It is sure, safe, stable, secure, unfailing, effective, trustworthy, and absolute. The testimony is sure. Therefore, we can be wise. As I grew into my teens, I already had established a relationship with

Jesus Christ. When I entered that period of seeking questions and answers, I developed in my education. The Bible was a resource and absolute truth in my life. I began to rely on what I learned. My code of ethics was found in His Word because it works.

"The statutes of the Lord are right, rejoicing the heart" (Psalm 19:8a). The Bible is God's story and is a document of importance. It is His rule for us. The precepts of God's Word are founded in His righteousness. His Word is not polluted or diluted. I have confidence in His Word for it is right. In my adulthood, I have had many opportunities to share the Word. In this book, I have shared some of the blessings. It has been a difficult time. The enemy has been throwing darts at me. I started keeping a record of God's intervention. The column of rejoicing surpasses the attacks. His Word has been used against the enemy and has also been the answer for my seeking heart. I am appreciative to the Lord in providing the Scripture. Claim it for your life, sit back and watch it work.

"The commandment of the Lord is pure, enlightening the eyes" (Psalm 19:8a). My life has been recreated and transformed through His Word.

As simple as I am, the Word has provided a sure testimony. It has demolished the enemy through the power of God's Word (2 Corinthians 10:5). It is a sacred book and has brought much joy and peace. My eyes have been enlightened through His Word. In my older years, I have set my mind on things above. I think the writing of my book has challenged me to think about praiseworthy things. The promise I started this chapter with "He that followeth after righteousness and mercy findeth life, righteousness and honor" (Proverbs 21:21), has worked for me and will for you. Is He calling you? Listen! Can you hear His voice? Please follow Him.

TWENTY ONE

BLESSED ASSURANCE
Colossians 1:27

The songwriter has written, "Blessed assurance, Jesus is mine; this is my story, this is my song, praising my Savior all the day long; this is my story, this is my song." As I have been writing *Discovering God's Favor*, grace has been amazing. "All is at rest, happy and blessed, watching and waiting, looking above." I find myself lost in his love. I have prayed that God would extend my ministries through our children. I have had to learn that God will get his desires and goals accomplished. I do not have to be the one to do it for Him. I have always been a doer. If the job needs to get done, I will do it. Sometimes I have pushed ahead of schedule with a sincere heart to do the right thing and sometimes the schedule was not God's. I have prayed with passion and have pursued His will with intensity. I have taken risks and made big and small mistakes. I have been forgiven. I am now sitting down and watching God's hand at work. Both of our children have expanded our goals to glorify God through their continued life and work experiences. I have always had a sensitive heart and discerning spirit to help people. Teaching and counsel have gone hand-in-hand and is now carried on through our son's ministry as an educator, guidance counselor and principal. Until now, I have never sat in one place long enough to see how God has taken him to a place of extended possibilities of service. It is a delight to observe and dream the future into place. What is coming? Only God knows. We are watching in anticipation. Sarah, John's wife, has been a joy to our hearts. She is very relational; her ongoing personality will bring many opportunities to extend our ministries. They have ministered in the country of Turkey and have visited the seven churches referenced in the Revelation. Their contribution as servants of Jesus Christ will continue to glorify our Lord Jesus Christ. They have four children, and it is a joy to watch them grow. Each one has something to contribute to the cause of Christ. We delight in seeing them magnify Jesus' name in their own unique ways. Today in 2015, they can be described by many words: Cameron is persistent and focused, Analise is sensitive and bright in her studies, Elaina is passionate and creative and Isaiah is playful and is adopted from Ethiopia. They are a picture of joy.

I have always loved the church and felt called to serve its Founder. I have a deep love for Jesus Christ. Without Him, I am nothing. With Him, I am everything. God is accomplishing His will through us. Our daughter, Amy, has carried on the detailed administration leadership role. She has learned to carry out the projects and is proclaiming the word of truth through the pastors she works with. With excitement, we look to the future and watch and wait to see God's handiwork. She has adopted two daughters from Ethiopia. Aliya is an over-achiever, diligent and energetic and Jocelyn is irresistibly spirited. With Amy's optimistic spirit, the trio is a great delight to be around. There is always excitement and challenge.

I have included myself in the Scripture that says,

"I have no greater joy than to hear that my children and grandchildren are walking in the truth." My prayer is that we will be all that God intends us to be through faith, hope and love. Radical life begins with the promise that I exist for God and for His purpose, not my own. My aim is to glorify God in all things. We know the world is soiled but we need to open our doors to our neighborhoods and get out of the 'Christian ghetto.'

Faith will get us started because it makes us available. We want to see a transformation of our communities. Our calling is to be in the world without living according to the elementary principles of a fallen world. This is my story given to share God's presence. We are human beings and we are material and immaterial, flesh and spirit, visible and invisible. We are part of two spheres, earth and heaven. We are not to fix our eyes on what is seen which is temporary but on what is unseen, as that is eternal (2 Corinthians 4:18).

Hope leads us to responsibility. Hope is confidence in whom we believe in. A response is necessary. We accept our limitations while dreaming of the unlimited redemption we have received.

Radical life is committed to drawing others to God. Simplicity and silence will drown out the noise and lead us to God's presence. Life will become a slowing-up process and a running track simultaneously. We are able to be responsible in our response.

Love is a result of faith and hope. It leads us to accountability. Storytelling is necessary. As I tell my story, it will lead me to hearing others. Our calling is to be human and bring glory to God. We are all unique and have special stories to tell. We are called to live out the gospel using our gifts, talents and skills to bless others and glorify God. I am excited to watch and hear the redemptive conversation of each family member.

TWENTY TWO

BE STILL MY SOUL
Psalm 46:10

The songwriter has written, "Be still, my soul, the Lord is on my side; bear patiently the cross of grief or pain; leave to thy God to order and provide, in every change He faithful will remain." To be still and know that "I am God" will help me see my past, present and future from the perch of an eternal now. God is above time. If all now is for God, I can live out my clock time with joyous anticipation. As my spiritual autobiography comes to the end, where do I go from here? It seems like I have mentioned many subjects. It started like a history book with many facts and dates. Next, a study on conversion and theological birth concept was written, not too deep but hopefully understandable. Childhood and adolescent development followed, with a central focus on God's faithfulness and education, and its lifelong journey that started so many years ago and continues on. The triple-torch career started at age 16 and after 50 years is still moving forward. The family is working together with love and growth in grace. After all of those activities, I could have had a mental and physical breakdown, but instead it has been a challenging, edifying and exciting glorious adventure.

"Be still and know that I am God." What is the 'now' going to have for me? How can I prepare for my eternal destiny? How can I actually make my daily decisions in an eternal, heavenly-directed way? I know the 'doing' for Jesus will find its proper place when the 'being' is in focus. It is a bigger-than-life pursuit. He is living His life through me. If I fail, I am going to bounce right back on the wagon. As the Holy Spirit pulls me up the street of life, he will produce the right attitude and create the appropriate character in me. This is the plan of action to follow for me, and if you are interested, apply it to yourself.

I discovered that I must first be still. Simplicity

and silence will drown out the noise and lead me to God's presence. It is good to be busy, not lazy. It is good to be active, not slothful. Sometimes I have learned that doing should be placed in silence. We should observe what God is accomplishing. I have been too busy to see. He says, "Be still." What joy is brought to our souls when we are confronted with a problem which has no solution, and yet God works it out for our own good and His glory! It is good for us, on occasion, just to stand still and watch the mighty hand of God intently. When we do, we can say that the Lord of hosts is with us. God is telling me to be still and wants me to enter into a period of tranquility. 'Observing' is watching with a careful eye, someone or something. He wants me to see His mighty hand. I must have zeal in my walk. I must have a soul that is earnest. I must have spiritual fervency.

In being still, I have discovered that God is working in me both to will and to do His good pleasure. I am realizing that God is the one continually and effectually working in me. I am His workmanship. The Holy Spirit dwelling within makes the abundant life a reality, not merely a possibility. The energy of God enables me to desire His will. The divine sovereignty is at work. As I reach up to Him, I am learning how to bring my will into submission. He says 'pursue holiness if you want to be near me.' "Be ye holy for I am holy." This means that I must pray, "Create in me a clean heart" (Psalm 51:10). He says, "Yield your members to righteousness and holiness" (Romans 6:19). Righteousness must become my master. How am I going to do this? He says, "Watch over your heart with diligence" (Proverbs 4:23). I must become God-centered, not self-centered, in regard to sin. Sin is offensive, grievous and disobedient to God.

The plan of action is to be still, be His workmanship and be blameless. Following the plan is not a formula or set of requirements to meet; it is a product of obedience.

The 'now' for me is having daily interaction with God. I need him and am dependent upon Him. I am helpless without Him. I realize this need through a correct estimate of myself and through being honest with myself. I need to know myself and accept myself and be in complete submission to Him. Confession of the believing heart is the initial decision. In faith, the possession of God's power enables me to live in Christ Jesus with enthusiasm. I have to learn to live life and be real; I have to uncover my sin. I need to see sin as God does and treat it the way He does. I need to confess my daily sins as He makes them known to me. I need to be sorry for the dysfunctional lifestyle. A conscious awareness of His presence will cause the repenting spirit.

I need to recognize that the divine participates with me. I am not alone. I am able to pursue every activity with a quiet heart because Jesus is working through me. He gives the confidence that we have power through His partnership. He can fix the situation immediately and will eventually. I have learned that mastering righteousness comes through relinquishing my will to the Holy Spirit. I have a driving force and compelling motivation to experience a Christ-like life. As I seek with diligence and as I surrender and obey, I will become what God wants me to become. When my mind condition is correct, my outward condition will demonstrate love, faith and hope. My interaction with God through Jesus Christ and the assistance of the Holy Spirit will produce wonderful results. A daily routine with others will begin with a contagious, caring heart that is tender, kind, gracious, agreeable and sharing. I will become a channel of God's mercy. Problems of others will become mine and cared-for in like manner.

My dependence and reliance on God continue to be demonstrated. The cleansing of impurities gives me freedom to help others. The pure in heart have an intuitive sense of God's leading because a re-education of behavioral problems has begun. The molding of character takes place as we become more dependent. Everyone is looking for internal peace that is generated through our relationship with Jesus Christ. God's intervention will ultimately bring peace. If we are in harmony with God, we will have peace that will be seen through our daily activities. My daily routine with others will bring some suffering. Jesus doesn't promise ease to those called to follow Him. Reliance upon Jesus will cause radical living. Ridicule will most likely pursue us but keep in mind that rewards will follow. Jesus lived through persecution, He died through persecution and He rose again after the persecution. If you want to find a deep, real and forever happiness, wrap yourself around Christ.

TWENTY THREE

HAVE THINE OWN WAY LORD
Philippians 3:10

The songwriter has written, "Have Thine Own Way, Lord! Have Thine Own Way! Hold o'er my being absolute sway! Fill with thy spirit till all shall see, Christ only always living in me!" Time has slipped by so fast. I have reviewed God's greatness, goodness and graciousness. It's time to bring you up-to-date; I need to give a glimpse of the present. Faith, hope and love continue to shine through God's grace in my life. The end opens the way to eternity. This history has a beginning without an end, only a departure from this earth to heaven. My daily goal is to be contagious, with a heart that is tender, gracious, agreeable and sharing. This challenge will be demonstrated through my dependence and reliance on God. I want everyone to wrap themselves around Christ.

Living in the "now" is important to me. I want to know Christ more. I want to experience His power more. I want to spend more time in fellowship with Him. I want to endure suffering in Him more. I want to experience dying to self more. (Philippians 3:10). I want to know Christ more. This means to have a personal relationship with Him through faith (John 17:3). Receiving Christ is the first decision (John 1:12). Learning to know Him should be the second decision (2 Peter 3:18). This will become a life pursuit.

Jesus Christ was God himself wrapped in human flesh (John 1:1, 14). "He is the image of the invisible God...For God was pleased to have all His fullness dwell in Him" (Colossians 1:15, 19). This is what I celebrate each year at Christmas. Jesus left heaven's glory and came to live on earth to save me from my sin. He wants to blot sin and guilt from my soul and implant His life within me by the Holy Spirit. Through His death and resurrection, He made salvation possible. Jesus was my sacrifice for sin. He was my substitute. He deliberately endured God's judgment and wrath for me. The cross deals with God's judgment for my sin. God made Him who had no sin to be sin for me (2 Corinthians 5:21). By His death He frees me from sin's dominion and brings me into His family (Matthew 20:28). He is my redeemer. Christ triumphed over all the forces of evil and death and hell (Colossians 2:15). Satan has been defeated and Christ is the victor!

People come to Christ in many different ways. Some conversions are sudden and dramatic, a radical change from one way of living to another. Others come to Christ slowly with the crossing over from unbelief to belief. My heart's desire is to follow my family's encounter with Christ and observe their redemptive story.

I want to experience His power more. I want to allow Christ, through obedience, to live in me (Galatians 2:20). It's hard to believe, but God Himself comes to live within me by the Holy Spirit. I am not alone, God is with me! In fact, even before I believed, His spirit was already working in me by conviction of sin and drawing me to Himself. The Holy Spirit lives permanently within me (Romans 8:9). I am His temple (1 Corinthians 6:19). He gives me a new life, new relationship, new citizenship, new destiny and a new family. My decision for Christ isn't an end but a beginning. He walks with me. God has actually taken up residence within me. I may not always feel different or be aware of His presence but Jesus' promise to His disciples has already been fulfilled: "I will ask the Father and He will give you another counselor to be with you forever – the Spirit of truth" (John 14:16-17). Someone once said, "I need Jesus Christ for my eternal life and the Holy Spirit of God for my *internal* life." Jesus said, "Flesh gives birth to flesh but the spirit gives birth to spirit" (John 3:6). The Holy Spirit has been given to help me become more like Christ. I become more like Christ as I claim His promises on a daily basis. As I grow in His grace and knowledge, my character will reflect Christ. My actions and attitudes will be a bright light for Him. This takes place when I deliberately turn from sin and He fills my spirit, soul and body (Psalm 139:23-24). I must be submissive (Luke 9:23). I have to commit every area of my life to His authority. I must obey and trust Him. I have to do what He wants me to do because I know that His way is right (Psalm 119:101).

I want to have fellowship with Him more. He is not only my Savior, friend and companion but my Lord. The words 'discipline' and 'disciple' resemble each other in the English language. The most common word in the Gospel for a Christian is 'disciple'. It takes discipline of the mind, discipline of the soul and discipline of the spirit to be a disciple. To live in fellowship with Jesus Christ involves discipleship. In Jesus' day, the word would be known. Many philosophers and teachers gathered students around them. If I am going to have close fellowship with Jesus, I must become a learner or a student. Personal relationships take time to develop. The disciples walked with Him, ate with Him, conversed with Him, observed His life and listened to Him preach and teach. I must learn from Him. I like studying. In my full time ministries, I prepared many sermons and I enjoyed every minute of that preparation. Today I spend time doing research and study just to get closer to Jesus and to know him better. The psalmist was right, "the unfolding of your word gives light, it gives understanding to the simple" (Psalm 119:130).

This book was written primarily for my own personal growth. Not only is a disciple a learner but also a follower. To follow Jesus is to follow His teaching. Jesus said, "You are my friend if you do what I command" (John 15:14). I have to learn what Jesus is teaching and then I have to put the instruction into action. In every situation in my life, I have to think about what Jesus would do. I believe in life-long learning. It should be a challenge for everyone. Learning and following Jesus will cause intimacy with Him.

I want to endure suffering in Him more. I have had some painful opportunities. The attack of the enemy is hard but the victory is rewarding. The Christian life isn't a playground but a battlefield. I have faced many roadblocks. Following Christ will not bring relief or freedom from problems. It will bring peace with God through the problems (John 14:27). It is an inner peace that comes from a deep and abiding trust in His promises. I have peace with God through my reception of Jesus Christ (Romans 5:1). In this world, I have experienced troubles and I have to keep in mind that if the enemy persecuted Jesus, they will persecute me (John 15:20). But through it all, He gives comfort and inner peace. The conflict is a spiritual force of evil (Ephesians 6:12). Satan is real and he will do everything he can to pull us away from God. He wants to bring discouragement and make us weak and ineffective.

The key to spiritual victory is to stay close to God. I have to turn every area of my life over to Him. This means to renounce control over my life and to hand my soul over to His authority. I have to practice God's presence all day long. The Bible tells me to "pray continually" (I Thessalonians 5:17). My favorite Scripture when in trouble is Psalm 145:18, "The Lord is near to all who call on Him." In the stormy times of life, I am not in a helpless or hopeless situation. I have a choice every day either to come near to God or drift away from Him. I want to experience dying to self more and allowing Him to live through me. A lifestyle through the death process involves real living. This is not negative thinking but a positive approach to daily activities. I die to self when I look at earth from heaven's point of view. I have to occupy my mind with eternal values. This involves a "clean heart" (Psalm 51:10). "For out of the heart comes evil thoughts" (Matthew 15:19). My mind and body are closely linked. The reflection of inner thoughts will be displayed by my behavior. I have to learn to live "free from accusation" (Colossians 1:21-22). God wants me to act justly and to love mercy and walk humbly with Him. As I walk humbly with Him, confrontation, confession and contentment will follow. I will confront the weakness and will confess unrighteous acts to Him. I will experience death to self and contentment in living.

Dying to self involves having a guarded heart (Proverbs 4:23). Satan doesn't attack the strong and fortified points in my life. He goes after the weaknesses in character, unconfessed sin and harmful habits in order to invade and bring destruction. I have to learn to stand firmly on God's promises. "The Lord is with me, I will not be afraid" (Psalm 118:6). He will sustain me (Psalm 55:22). He cares for me and He will not leave me (Hebrews 13:5). Through dying to self, I can trust my life to the promise giver (2 Peter 1:4) because He protects and sustains my heart.

This involves having a persistent heart. God doesn't want me to coast along in life. He doesn't want a self-satisfied, stagnant life. He wants my heart to spend time with Him. He wants me to commit my way to Him. He wants me to trust in Him. He will then shine brightly through me (Psalm 37:5, 6). The

Bible says, "For you were once in darkness, but now you are light in the Lord. Live as children of light" (Ephesians 5:8-11). Every moment belongs to Jesus.

Dying to self involves having a knowledgeable heart. The Bible says, "I will instruct you and teach you in the way you should go; I will counsel you and watch over you" (Psalm 32:8). I don't have to rely upon myself for direction. Bad choices don't have to follow my path. God knows all about me. He knows what is best for me. He sees the dangers that I face and He also knows the joys that I could experience. I have to learn to not run my own life. God loves me and has a plan for my life. I have to commit my decisions to God. "Teach me your way...give me an undivided heart" (Psalm 81:11). He wants me to seek His will and wants me to discover His will and then He wants me to do it. The Bible says, "A man's heart reflects the man" (Proverbs 27:19).

My prayer is "Have thine own way, Lord." The 'now' is very active. The goal is to know Jesus. I take great joy in following my grandchildren's redemptive story. Listening to their prayers, observing their actions, and delighting in conversation with in direct questioning have brought happiness in following their journey of faith.

The goal is to experience Jesus' power. It is always a happy time when my children have witnessed His power through promises fulfilled. There are always times of new challenges. In this day of depression, desperation and discontent, they have learned how to participate with God's hands. The goal is to have more fellowship. Jesus is a live-in companion. In my marriage, I have a oneness, a togetherness, that strives to grow in a steady intimate fellowship with God and with one another. I celebrate life in magnifying Jesus' name. The goal is to suffer in Jesus' name. As I draw near to God, He will draw near to me. "Thy will be done" is always the response. He has my best interest in mind whether I understand or not. Dying to self gets me out of the picture. It places Jesus in His rightful place. Another man named John said Jesus must increase and I must decrease. The key model to follow is "Above All, Jesus."

TWENTY FOUR

FATHER, WE LOVE YOU
John 12:28; Matthew 6:13

The songwriter has written, "Father, we love you, we worship you and adore you, glorify Thy name." The Bible says, "For Thine is the kingdom and the power and the glory forever, Amen" (Matthew 6:13). In these words, we find the assurance that all we need is available to us through Jesus Christ. We must learn to put faith into action through submission, obedience and trust. We are able to do this because God is great, powerful, glorious, victorious and majestic. All that is in the heaven and in the earth is His. "O Lord, thou art exalted as head above all" (I Chronicles 29:11). Faith is a decision to trust in God's Word. It deals with a spiritual quality of an individual. Each individual has to reject or receive this truth. It is a decision of the will to respond to the Scripture, "but as many as received Him, to them gave He the power to become the children of God, even to them that believe on His name" (John 1:12). It is not simply the assent of the intellect but a practical submission of the entire man - spirit, soul, body - to the truth. If we receive the divine testimony and yield to it, we become partakers of heavenly knowledge (Luke 8:10, John 8:31, 32). I have entrusted my being to the facts of Scripture and have a growing, personal relationship with Jesus Christ.

The faith factor leads to submission to Jesus in whom I have entrusted my spirit, soul and body. Submission means to surrender, yield and obey. I have to present my life as a sacrifice to Jesus Christ. It is not a mindless fluttering of the heart but is the presentation of an entire life to the Lord (Romans 12:1, 2). I have to learn to live out the new creation I possess in Jesus Christ (2 Corinthians 5:17). My life is not governed by the thought patterns and dictates of this evil world system. The transformation in my inward nature will bring glory to my heavenly Father.

I find it amazing that the "Lord's prayer"

begins with "hallowed be Thy name" and ends with "for Thine is the glory." In the introduction and doxology, it starts and finishes with His reverence, honor, worship and majesty, awe and glory. God is worthy of all the attention, praise, honor and service that we could ever give to Him. The word "glory," whether in the Old or New Testament, refers to the excellency of God's person, His great acts and to the many aspects of His merciful kindness to His people. David expressed His thanksgiving to God in I Chronicles 16:10, 24, 27, 35. Moses gives testimony in Exodus 33:13, 14, 18, 19; 34:6. There is nothing so great, so good, so valuable, so important and so worthy of worship, praise and adoring sacrifice as the Person of God Himself (I Chronicles 29:10,11). In the Bible, the "glory of God" refers to the divine manifestation in the person of the Lord Jesus Christ. Jesus Christ became a member of the human race as God's prophet, priest and king. In Jesus Christ, in His person, work and words, we find the very character of God (Hebrews 1:1-3). "We behold His glory...the only begotten of the Father" (John 1:14).

When I pray "for Thine is the kingdom and the power and glory forever, Amen," it motivates me to live for God's glory. This means to initiate the attitude of worship, praise and thanksgiving and then to practice that attitude. I have to learn to choose to initiate and maintain an attitude that is in harmony with God's greatness and goodness (I Chronicles 16:23-29, 34). The glory of God in my life begins with praying for it. I must retain the goal to glorify Him. The Scripture says, "and whatsoever ye shall ask in my name, that will I do, that the Father may be glorified in the Son" (John 14:13). Jesus Christ says "Thy will be done". When I can say, "not my will but yours", I will be living out I Corinthians 10:31, "whether therefore ye eat or drink or whatsoever ye do, do all to the glory of God." My prayer is "teach me Thy way, O Lord, I will walk in Thy truth, unite my heart to fear Thy name – I will praise thee, O Lord my God, with all my heart and I will glorify Thy name for evermore" (Psalm 86:11, 12).

When I understand what it means to "hallow His name" and give glory to His name, the result will be reverence and exaltation. This means that my life will be in harmony with God. It will develop a way of life to produce good works. "Let your light so shine before men that they may see your good works and glorify your Father which is in heaven" (Matthew 5:16). The term "good works" simply refers to actions which may be described as good. This would include those characterized by honesty, mercy, righteousness, kindness, gratitude, love and patience. It would be a life of unity. "Now the God of patience and consolation grant you to be like-minded one toward another according to Christ Jesus, that ye may with one mind and one mouth glorify God, even the Father of our Lord Jesus Christ" (Romans 15:5, 6). We are united in Jesus Christ and there is no confusion, division or disunity.

We should have a life of purity. "What? Know ye not that your body is the temple of the Holy Ghost, which is in you, which ye have of God, and ye are not your own? For ye are bought with a price, therefore glorify God in your body, and in your spirit which are God's" (I Corinthians 6:19, 20). We belong to God. He lives in us. We must aggressively live day by day to the glory of God. We have been given divine enablement to serve God. "As every man hath received the gift…that God by all things may be glorified through Jesus Christ" (I Peter 4:10, 11). We can dispense the grace of God through a ministry of the Word of God.

I can glorify God through the life of Christ living in and through me. This is a priority for life. Every activity, every thought and every bit of energy has to be integrated with the presence of "Our Heavenly Father." This can be accomplished through the process of reconstruction, which is growth in grace.

CONCLUSION

AMAZING GRACE
Ephesians 1:7

The songwriter has written, "Amazing Grace! How sweet the sound! Thru many dangers, toils and snares... and grace my fears relieved...'tis grace that brought me safe thus far, and grace will lead me home." According to God's grace, I have been redeemed and forgiven (Ephesians 1:7). "The earth shall soon dissolve like snow, the sun forbear to shine, but God, who called me here below, shall be forever mine." *Discovering God's Favor* is in its second printing in 2015. It has been driven by passion, independence and diversity. Its foundation has been built on God's greatness seen in His sovereignty. His goodness has been seen in His blessings. His grace has been shared through each chapter in my spiritual autobiography. The journey of faith is a story of my growing in the grace and knowledge of our Lord and Savior Jesus Christ (2 Peter 3:18). The purpose has always been to glorify God by putting His character, His will and His ways into action (2 Corinthians 3:18).

I have been blessed by God the Father (Ephesians 1:4-6). He has chosen me (1:4). God in His love seeks the sinner (Luke 19:10). He has chosen me in Christ, it is not in myself. The mystery of divine sovereignty and human responsibility will never be solved in this life. Both are taught in the Bible (John 6:37). The beginning of faith, trust and belief in Jesus Christ, came to me through these words, "Come unto me" (Matthew 11:28-30). Sin is living independently from God. Salvation begins with humility and total dependence on God. It involves turning around in my mind. It is a heart-knowledge. Submission to the truth and complete reliance is necessary. Read about my conversion in Chapter 2 *Only Trust Him.* I am discovering how to shine with His character. It takes daily decision, determination, dedication and discipline.

I have been blessed by God the Son (Ephesians

1:9-12). He has redeemed me. To redeem means to purchase and set free by paying a price. I am free from the law (Galatians 5:1), free from slavery to sin (Romans 6) and free from the power of Satan and the world (Galatians 1:4, Colossians 1:13-14). I am able to live the Biblical spiritual Christian life because of my redemption. I use the word 'biblical' because the authority comes from God's Holy Word. I use the word 'spiritual' because the Holy Spirit indwells me. It is possible because of His enablement. I use the word 'Christian' because the Lord Jesus Christ is my Savior, Lord, prophet, priest and king. I am able to live with His divine residence, divine transformation and divine will (Romans 12:1, 2). Read about my transformation in Chapter 8, 'Lamb of Glory'. I am learning to live in His will. It takes affirmation, acceptance, adjustment and assurance.

I have been blessed by God the Holy Spirit (Ephesians 1:13-14). He has sealed me (1:13). I have accepted the good news that Christ died for my sin, was buried and rose again (I Corinthians 15:1). His sealing means ownership. God has put His seal upon me because He has purchased me to be His own (I Corinthians 6:19-20). It also means security and protection. According to John 14:16-17, the Holy Spirit abides with the believer forever. The seal is a mark of authenticity. I have been redeemed through faith in Jesus Christ (Ephesians 1:7). I have been redeemed as the Spirit works in me to make me more like Christ. I shall be redeemed when Christ returns and I become like Him.

This is the last chapter of my book but it is not the end of my story. My life on earth is only the preparation for eternity. Several years ago, in 2006, I celebrated my 50th year in ministry. I prayed for further service. To my surprise, through sickness, I was provided a new challenge. A pastoral health care initiative has taken place. I have integrated pastoral interest into health issues providing a spiritual solution strategy. I have enjoyed doing research projects. My life has been a life-long learning experience. It has become a natural part of my journey. When unexpected heart disease, cancer and other internal problems came into my life, my goal is to find a spiritual, psychological and physical solution. The research produced my 'Discovering God' book series and 'Pastoral Prescription' cards, a spiritual solution for visitation needs. The research prepared me to accept the invitation to be a visitation pastor. This has provided many opportunities to minister. After a few years making house calls, hospice care was added to the pastoral health care initiative. I do not know what is in the future but I know who holds the future. The Holy Spirit has sealed me. I am going to minister where I am. I will continue in His way to glorify Him and live by His grace. *Discovering God's Favor* has been an exciting experience. It will continue with 'Discovering God's Presence', 'Discovering God's Heart', and 'Discovering God's Blessings'. Have you experienced the amazing grace of Jesus?

ACKNOWLEDGEMENTS

I appreciate all the people that God has used to influence me. Many of these thoughts have come to my memory over the past seventy-five years through sermon notes, lectures, conversations, meditations and reading. I have not knowingly withheld any significant reference from others in my devotional. To the best of my knowledge, all statements and information are true and correct and given credit. Everyone I have come in contact with should be given credit. The devotional is a constant source of strength, support and security for me and I hope also for you.

SOURCES

All songs are taken from: Peterson, John W., *Great Hymns of the Faith*, Singspiration Inc., Grand Rapids, Michigan 1968 unless indicated. All Scripture is taken from: Authorized King James Version and New International Version unless indicated. References made from Exposition on Matthew 11:28-30, MacArthur, John F. Jr., *The Gospel According to Jesus*, Zondervan, Grand Rapids, Michigan 1994. References made from Exposition on Psalm 23:1-6, Evans, Anthony T., *Our God is Awesome*, Moody Press, Chicago, Illinois 1994. Words from the song "I'd Rather Have Jesus", *The Celebration Hymnal*, Word Music 1997. References made on premarital advice, Wright, H. Norman, *So You're Getting Married*, Regal Books, Ventura, California 1985. Words from the song, His Very Own, Cox, Sidney E.,

Source unknown. References made from p. 184-248, Allender, Dan B., *The Healing Path*, Waterbrook Press, Colorado Springs, Colorado 1999. References made from p. 137,142, Wiersbe, Warren W., *Be Hopeful*, SP Publications Inc., Wheaton, Illinois 1982. References made from pg 6-7, Arthur, Kay, Harvest House Publishers, Eugene, Oregon 1955. References made from pgs 48-51, Temple, Joe, *He Ascended Into Heaven*, Good News Broadcaster, Back to the Bible Broadcast, Lincoln, Nebraska 1982. References made from pgs 77-92, Evans, Tony, *Our God Is Awesome*, Moody Press, Chicago, Illinois 1993. References made from pgs 125-146, Torrey, R.A., *The Power of Prayer*, Zondervan Publishing House, Grand Rapids, Michigan 1955. References made from pgs 9-25, Weiss, Christian G., *Praying With Authority*, Back to the Bible Broadcast, Lincoln, Nebraska 1965. References made from lecture notes, Matthew, Victor M., "The Biblical Measure of Success: The Glory of God", Grand Rapids, Michigan. References made from pgs 26-28, Wilson, Bill, Josh McDowell, *A Ready Defense*, Thomas Nelson Inc., Nashville, Tennessee 1993. References made from pages 1100 and 2440, Falwell, Jerry, *Liberty Bible Commentary*,

Old Time Gospel Hour, Thomas Nelson, Inc., Nashville, Tennessee 1983.

ABOUT THE AUTHOR

John F. Gillette, D.Min., has pursued a life-long learning adventure. It has been diversified. It has been traditional, alternative and innovative. It has always produced new possibilities and caused proficiency. *Discovering God's Favor* is his spiritual autobiography. It was written to celebrate his fiftieth anniversary in ministry (from ages 16-66). It was produced to remind himself of God's greatness, goodness and graciousness. It was published to share insights into many important life issues with his family and others (see Topical Index). His philosophy in life has always been God, family and ministry. He is proud of his wife, Joy, son, John and daughter, Amy and the grandchildren, Cameron, Analise, Elaina, Aliya, Isaiah and Jocelyn. His love for them will always be present. His prayer for the family and others that read this testimony is expressed in Psalm 42:2, 8, "My soul thirsteth for God, for the living God, when shall I come and appear before God? The Lord will command His lovingkindness in the daytime and in the night His song shall be with us." His model has been Jesus Christ. "I have set the Lord always before me; because He is at my right hand, I shall not be moved" (Psalm 16:8). His intense interest in the Word of God has pursued his daily activities as a musician, minister and mentor. This testimony provides a confirmation that God's grace is real and abundant, "Above All, Christ" (John 3:31).

CPSIA information can be obtained
at www.ICGtesting.com
Printed in the USA
FFOW03n2215131015
17674FF